Stirling moss
GREAT DRIVES
In the Lakes & Dales

~

Stirling moss
GREAT DRIVES
In the Lakes & Dales

~

Colin shelbourn

with photography by David ward

Little, Brown and Company

Boston   New York   Toronto   London

Page one: The Keswick boat landing-stage at Crow Park, Derwent Water.
Pages two and three: Sheep at Malham Cove, Yorkshire Dales.
This page: Just after sunset on Thirlmere.

A Little, Brown book

Text copyright © 1993 by Colin Shelbourn
Photographs copyright © 1993 by David Ward
Designed by Gary Ottewill
Cartography by Pam Grant

First published in 1993
This paperback edition published in 1998
ISBN 0 316 64535 4
A CIP catalogue record for this book is available from the British Library.

Typeset by Hewer Text Composition Services, Edinburgh
Colour separations by Fotographics, Hong Kong
Printed in Italy by Amilcare Pizzi spa, Milan

Little, Brown and Company (UK)
Brettenham House, Lancaster Place
London WC2E 7EN

CONTENTS

~

Introduction by Stirling Moss
pages 9 to 11

Opposite: An early morning view of Grasmere from Loughrigg Terrace.

INTRODUCTION

~

I first learnt to drive when I was about six. Perched on my dad's knee I used to drive the family car down the long drive of our farm at Bray, beside the River Thames. By the age of ten, I had my first car; an ancient Austin Seven, which father bought for £15. My first real road car was an air-cooled Morgan three wheeler, which was my pride and joy when I was fifteen. Two years later, I was allowed to take over my father's 1940 MG TB Tickford Coupé.

Since then, I have raced and driven innumerable cars and travelled all over the world, both for pleasure and through my business interests. Racing is now a hobby, rather than a profession, but I still greatly enjoy touring certain places by car. Nowadays my favourite car for sightseeing is my Mercedes 500SL convertible – in summer if the weather is good, it is wonderful – but almost any car will do as long as you are comfortable and can enjoy the drive.

I am not really a great walker and one of the reasons I first learnt to drive was because I could cover more ground and see more interesting places. We are fortunate in Britain that so much lovely countryside is easily accessible to the motorist. One of my favourite areas for touring is the north of England, especially the countryside of the Lake District and the Yorkshire Dales. There are few areas to beat it for sheer variety of landscape; in the course of a single afternoon's drive, you can encounter mountain passes, green valleys, open moor and wooded lake shores. The only other place I know offering such variety of scenery and ease of exploration is New Zealand.

Everyone has their own idea of what constitutes a good car tour, but for me there should be enough variety in road conditions and scenery to keep both driver and passengers entertained. The great thing about touring is that you don't need any expensive equipment or particular expertise – just a car you can rely on, a good guide book and map, and a sense of curiosity.

Great Drives in the Lakes and Dales features fifteen car tours which capture the best of a beautiful area. The routes range from two or three hour trips to longer expeditions which will take all day. We have aimed at a variety of routes to suit all drivers; not everyone wants to tackle one-in-four gradients and hairpin bends on their first trip. There is a lot to see and do within the Lake District and Yorkshire Dales but we have also chosen routes which venture outside the National Parks. These are ideal if you're caught up in holiday traffic – head out to the Solway Firth or the Forest of Bowland and you can be almost certain of quiet roads.

Whenever I visit the Lakes and Dales, I always find that the people are very friendly and go out of their way to be helpful. It is this sort of discovery which can make a car tour so pleasurable. For example, after a puncture on Hardknott Pass during my last trip to the Lakes, I was extremely grateful to find a garage owner in Eskdale who was willing to repair a tyre on a Sunday.

Another important aspect for me is the standard of accommodation and food. At the end of a journey I want to be able to relax at a comfortable hotel, in a friendly atmosphere. Some of the hotels and restaurants we've encountered have been excellent value, with wine lists which can be surprisingly good for a country area. So we have included recommendations for some of the smaller establishments which have a reputation for good food and hospitality. One vital tip – not every hotel takes credit cards, so make sure you pack your cheque book.

Whenever I embark on a trip I always make sure the car is well prepared before I set off. This is especially important in a country area where a car's average mileage per gallon can drop alarmingly and petrol stations may be few and far between. If you're returning late in the evening, bear in mind that even in quite large villages garages rarely stay open after 8.00 pm.

Another point to remember is that if you are trundling along at twenty miles per hour admiring the view, there may be someone behind who is in a hurry. Pull over when you can and let them past. You'll enjoy the view more if you can park somewhere and give passengers a chance to stretch their legs. In the individual tours, we've indicated the signs to follow with italics, to make them easy to spot as you drive. We've also suggested stopping places, viewpoints and even walks – although personally, I prefer to remain with the car delegating Susie, my wife, and our son Elliot when there is some reconnoitring to be done on foot!

Finally, enjoy your trip and I hope this book will be the starting point for many memorable journeys.

Happy touring!

Ciao,

The open road beside Crummock Water.

TOUR ONE
~
Caldbeck and
John Peel Country

This tour explores a relatively isolated

part of the Lake District National Park,

the wild moors beyond the northern fells,

Caldbeck Common and the area known

locally as 'Back o' Skiddaw'. Along the

route there are attractive villages,

magnificent views, the hunting ground of

the original John Peel and the home of

Tarzan's ancestors. . . .

Keswick to Caldbeck, via Bassenthwaite Lake and
Mirehouse and returning through Hesket Newmarket and
Greystoke, with a visit to Castlerigg Stone Circle.
Distance: 44 miles. Driving time: 3–4 hours

*Blencathra, also known as Saddleback
because of its distinctive shape.*

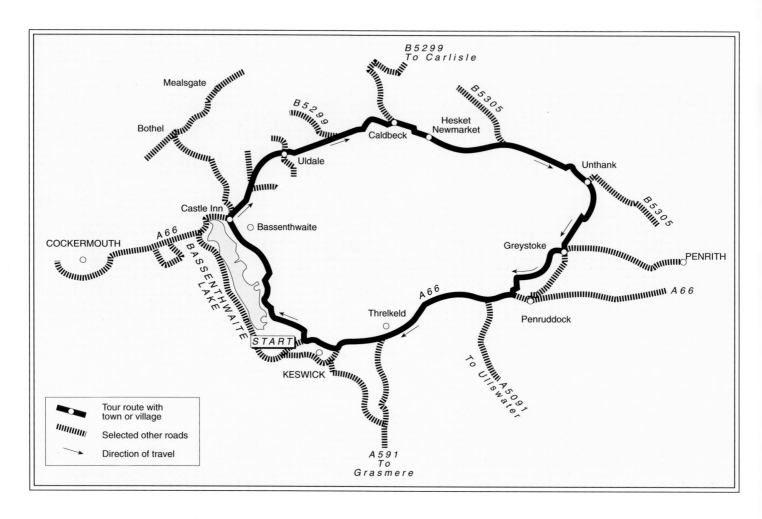

Tour route with town or village

Selected other roads

Direction of travel

KESWICK TO BASSENTHWAITE LAKE

Start at the Moot Hall information centre, in the centre of Keswick, and drive north, along Market Place, following the signs for *Cockermouth, Penrith* and *Keswick*. As you go over the River Greta, you pass the Cumberland Pencil Museum on your right.

Keswick is a former mining town which grew up following the discovery of copper ore in the Newlands Valley. Goldscope Mine was opened on 1 April 1565 and employed 50 German mining engineers from the newly-formed Company of the Mines Royal. This caused some resentment among the locals so, to avoid trouble, the miners lived on Derwent Island in the middle of Derwent Water. By the mid-seventeenth century copper had been superseded by graphite (or 'wad'), dug from the fells above Seathwaite, in Borrowdale. This was

used for a variety of purposes – from casting cannon balls to glazing pottery – until someone realized you could actually write with the stuff, and the Cumberland pencil industry was born.

Keswick has been a popular tourist resort since the late eighteenth century, although most of the town's buildings are Victorian. Tourism is still the town's main industry; there are more bed and breakfast establishments per head of the population than anywhere else in the country. The Moot Hall itself was built in 1813 as a market hall, and is a remarkable building, with its tower and its curious one-handed clock face.

Half a mile from the town centre, take the turning on the right (signed *Carlisle, Motorway* and *Penrith*) leading to a major roundabout. Go straight across (*Carlisle* and *Mirehouse*) and follow the A591 along one of its prettiest stretches as it runs beside Bassenthwaite Lake. There

Skiddaw is the Lake District's fourth highest mountain and also the oldest, being composed of sedimentary slate. It is one of the easiest to climb – unless you get caught in the mist.

are sixteen lakes in the Lake District but this is the only one which actually needs the word 'lake' in its title. The others are already called either 'water' or 'mere', hence the famous local joke: how many lakes are there in the Lake District? Answer: one.

Across the valley, on your left, rise the mountains of the Coledale Horseshoe. The bulk of Skiddaw looms on your right. This is the oldest (geologically speaking) of Lakeland's four 3,000ft peaks and it is certainly the easiest to climb; you can park almost half-way up. If you are determined to climb a mountain, this is probably the safest to attempt without full walking gear *as long as the weather is forecast to remain good.*

Left: Looking towards Threlkeld and the central Lakeland fells from Blencathra. Below: A resident at Priest's Mill; highly vocal and inclined to obstruct entry to the car-park.

by John Spedding, a contemporary of Wordsworth (they were at school together in Hawkshead). Tennyson stayed at Mirehouse whilst writing his version of the Arthurian legend, *Idylls of the King*. There's a small open-air theatre named after him by the edge of the lake. The Spedding family still owns Mirehouse, and you may be lucky enough to encounter them, guiding visitors around the public rooms. If you do, ask to hear the old cylinder recording of Tennyson reciting *The Charge of the Light Brigade*.

If the house is closed, there is a public footpath which leads through the fields to one of the most romantically sited churches in the country. St Bega's is a tiny Norman church which stands right beside the lake. Its origins may be pagan (the churchyard is circular and by running water) but it is named after an Irish noble lady who founded a Benedictine nunnery on the west coast – now called St Bees. When the valley was still thickly wooded and the lake was the major highway, worshippers were brought to the church by boat.

BASSENTHWAITE TO CALDBECK

Two and a half miles past Mirehouse you come to St John's Church and the turning for Bassenthwaite village. The village is not particularly scenic, so ignore the temptation to make a diversion, and carry on for another two miles until you come to the Castle Inn and a major crossroads. Turn right (*Uldale, Ireby and Caldbeck*) and you're on a very pleasant, tree-lined minor road. To begin with the views are limited to Binsey, the conical hill on your left (thought by connoisseurs to be the most boring fell in the Lakes), but have patience – the view soon opens up and you can see Skiddaw to your right. Look out for Whitewater Dash, the waterfall at the back of Skiddaw.

In spring the hedgerows along here are full of wild flowers. Keep to the road as it climbs on to the moors and then rolls

After a couple of miles, as you approach the lake, look across to the group of tiny white cottages on the fell beyond. Can you spot a white-painted rock, half-way up the crag below Lord's Seat? This is the famous Bishop of Barf. Legend has it that a bishop once tried to ride his horse up the screes to demonstrate his faith in God. The horse must have been a pagan because it fell and the bishop was killed. The rock is painted white by the landlord of the nearby hotel (although it did appear painted red, white and blue during the Queen's Silver Jubilee).

A mile further on, you come to Dodd Wood car-park and the Old Sawmill café. Mirehouse, just across the road, is highly recommended (but be sure to find out about opening times). It is a lovely English manor house, originally built as a hunting lodge by the eighth Earl of Derby in 1666. In 1802 it was bought

John Peel's grave in St Kentigern's churchyard, Caldbeck. His renown was such that the song was famous in his own lifetime, though to a different tune to the one we know now.

down to the tiny village of Uldale. Go straight through Uldale, past the Snooty Fox pub and back on to the moors. Soon there is another good view of Skiddaw, and if you look left you can see out to the Solway Firth. This is a very windswept moor but not a bad place for a picnic on a sunny day. The hills to your right are the Uldale Fells, one of which glories in the name Great Cockup (which, rather prosaically, turns out to be named after a nearby wood which once contained woodcocks). Look out for a very wind-swept tree on your left, just before you go over a tiny bridge; David Ward, our photographer, claims this is one of the most interesting trees in the Lake District!

You are now driving through the very attractive, rolling countryside of Cald-beck Common which leads down to Caldbeck village ('beck' is the local term for stream or river). The road goes over a cattle grid, past Parkend Restaurant, and bears left to enter the village. Look out for Swaledale Watch on your right – a good restaurant – and the large house with the odd name of Whelpo (just next to which is a house, dated 1698, which used to be a Methodist chapel). Follow the road into the centre of the village and about 100 yds past the Oddfellows Arms, look out for a wooden sign for Priest's Mill, just beyond St Kentigern's church.

A church was built here, by the River Cald, in 1118. Not much remains visible of the original twelfth-century building – the chancel was built in 1512, and the tower added in 1727 – but the church-yard has a couple of interesting residents: John Peel, born in 1777, who was master of the local fox hunt and became a legend in his own lifetime through the song *D'ye ken John Peel*, written by his friend, John Woodcott Graves of Cock-ermouth; and Mary Harrison, better known by her maiden name, Mary Robinson, who became famous as the Beauty of Buttermere. To learn more

about her you'll have to turn to the third tour.

Priest's Mill is worth a stop. It is a superbly converted corn mill which houses an excellent café, bookshop, art gallery and giftshop. The car park is tucked away behind the churchyard and is littered with ore trucks, rescued from Lake District mines. Each truck bears a brief historical note. Go round the back of the mill and you'll find the old water-wheel; put ten pence in the slot and you can watch it operate.

After a suitable stop for refreshments, extract your car from amongst all the hens and cockerels and continue along the road (left out of Priest's Mill). As you leave the village, you are greeted by a huge electricity generating windmill on the skyline to your left. You can get some idea of its scale by looking at the tree beside it; the span of the blades (from tip to tip) is around 113ft.

CALDBECK TO GREYSTOKE

Half a mile beyond Caldbeck, you reach Hesket Newmarket. As you enter the village, the rather dilapidated old build-ing on your left is Hesket Hall, which was built in the seventeenth century. Seen from the road, the house appears to be made up of peculiar angles and annexes. The story goes that it was built this way so that the shadows from the twelve corners of the building would act as a sundial.

Hesket Newmarket has an attractive village green and a covered market cross. On your right, as you leave the village, there's a small car-park. The Old Crown Inn is worth a visit. Whilst you're exploring, look for Dickens' House, just behind the market cross. Now a private house, it was originally the Queen's Head Inn, and Charles Dickens and Wilkie Collins stayed here during a walking tour in 1857.

Keep to the main road, following the

signs for *Penrith*. As you head through the very pastoral scenery, look back to the Lakes for a view of Carrock Fell and Bowscale Fell. Ahead of you are the Pennines; on one of the peaks is a white dot which turns out, prosaically, to be a British Airports Authority tracking station, and two summits to the left of it is Cross Fell, the highest point on the Pennine Way.

At the T-junction, four miles from Hesket Newmarket, turn right (*Penrith*) and join the B5305. A very straight stretch of road leads past a wireless receiving station and through the hamlet of Unthank. A mile beyond Unthank, you come to a sharp left-hand bend. You need to take the turning on the right (*Laithes, Blencow* and *Greystoke*), but if you continue along the main road, you can make a diversion to Hutton-in-the-Forest, home of Lord Inglewood and one of Cumbria's less well-known historic houses which is open to the public.

Having turned off the B5305, the minor road follows the line of the Hutton estate for a short period and you get a good view of Blencathra to your right (from this angle it is easy to see why it is also called Saddleback). As you pass through Little Blencow, look out for Blencow Hall, a pele tower which has a really attractive castellated farmhouse built on to it.

As you approach Greystoke, you'll start to follow a high wall on your right. This is the perimeter of the 6,000 acre Greystoke estate, one of the largest areas of enclosed private land in England. Past a few modern houses, and a house built into the wall, you come to the village centre and the green. The cross in front of you is Celtic, and the original manor house was built here by Lyulf, the Viking lord who gave his name to Ullswater.

The entrance to the Greystoke estate bears the coats of arms of the Grymthorpe and Howard families, but of course, as everyone knows, Greystoke was really the family name of Tarzan of the Apes. It's very unlikely that Edgar Rice Burroughs knew of the real Greystoke, but, in 1988, the centenary of Tarzan's fictitious birth, members of the British Edgar Rice Burroughs Society were invited to visit Greystoke Castle and were given a mock tour by the local vicar, who pointed out where various 'relatives' of the 'Lord of the Jungle' are buried in St Andrew's churchyard.

At the T-junction, opposite the school, turn right, then right again, on to the minor road for *Berrier*, just past the Boot and Shoe pub.

GREYSTOKE TO CASTLERIGG
The road follows the wall for a short period, then strikes off on its own, and a couple of miles beyond the village it

becomes very straight. This stretch runs parallel with an old Roman road which crosses the Greystoke estate through the fields on your right. After following the minor road for three miles, you come to another T-junction. Go left (*Troutbeck* and *Keswick*), and at the next T-junction, opposite the Sportsman Inn, go right, to join the A66. Turn right on to the A66 and you are heading back towards Keswick with more magnificent views of Blencathra and the Coledale Fells ahead.

Follow the A66 for six miles, past Threlkeld village, and look out for a small turning on your left, signed *St John's in the Vale Diocese Youth Centre* and *Castlerigg Stone Circle*. Take this turning and you are on the old main road.

CASTLERIGG TO KESWICK

Meandering uphill, you get a good view of St John's in the Vale on your left. After a mile, take the second turning on the left (*Castlerigg Stone Circle*). A few hundred yards beyond, take another left, to climb past a small wood. Three-quarters of a mile further on there is a small wooden signpost directing you to the stone circle. Park by the side of the road and go into the field if you want to see one of the best prehistoric sites in England. . . .

There are 48 stones, set in a circle roughly 90ft in diameter. The circle dates back perhaps 4,000 years and its exact purpose remains a mystery. Castlerigg is not as big as Stonehenge but its setting is far more spectacular; perched on a windswept plateau and surrounded by the Lakeland fells.

From Castlerigg, continue along the minor road back into Keswick. Turn left at the first T-junction, right at the next and back into the town centre. En route, you'll pass the Twa Dogs Inn, famous as the home of the legendary Boggart – half-badger, half-fox (if you don't believe me, they have a stuffed one in a glass case in the bar).

The countryside north of Keswick is so rarely explored by visitors to central Lakeland that it makes an excellent basis for a car tour. The roads are quiet, the scenery is rather special and you feel as though you're finding something new and exciting. One of the attractions is the unusual view of Skiddaw and Blencathra.

Standing above the village of Hesket Newmarket is a bit of man-made scenery – an electricity generating windmill. Whether you think it is an eyesore or not depends upon your point of view but I thought it suited the landscape quite well. It's privately owned and generates 400 kilowatts (that is enough to power around 200 domestic electric fires).

Commercial visitor attractions are few and far between but there are two good properties worth looking out for. Mirehouse is in a lovely location beside Bassenthwaite Lake, and it has a very friendly, unpretentious atmosphere. Hutton-in-the-Forest, towards Penrith, is on a slightly grander scale, and is perhaps more interesting for architecture buffs, though it is still quite laid-back in its approach to the visitor. Beware of the opening times at both these houses, by the way, as they are more restricted than some.

One property which isn't generally open to the public is Greystoke Castle. This is a shame because it is very impressive. It stands in the largest walled estate in England (some 6,500 acres). The castle is only open on special occasions, but the estate itself is run as a commercial enterprise, offering outdoor activities such as climbing, archery, shooting and rally karting, for corporate clients.

Finally, the short detour to Castlerigg Stone Circle is well worth making. This magnificent group of standing stones dates back to around 2,000 BC and is situated in the most stunning location. Get there when the sun is setting on a clear night and the view can be absolutely breath-taking.

Mirehouse, Bassenthwaite Lake.

TOUR TWO
~
The Langdales and Tarn Hows

A very pleasant half-day drive through
some of the best-known scenery in the
Lake District, including the countryside
associated with Beatrix Potter and a visit
to one of her homes, ending with a trip on
the ferry across Lake Windermere.

Windermere to Hawkshead and Sawrey, via the
Langdales, Coniston and Tarn Hows.
Distance: 33 miles. Driving time: 3 hours

Harrison Stickle with Millbeck Farm in the foreground.
The Langdale valley has been inhabited by man since Neolithic times.

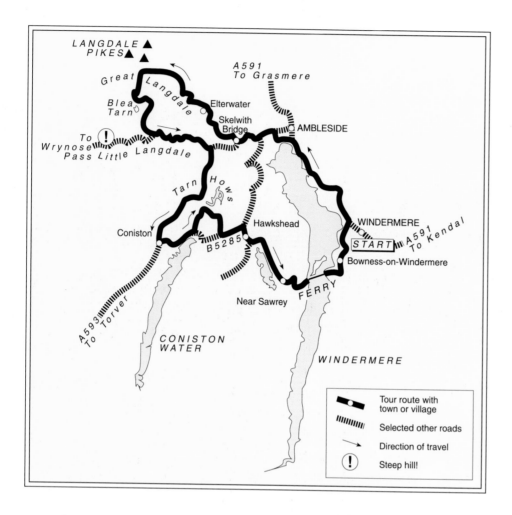

LANGDALE
PIKES▲ ▲
        ▲

Great Langdale

Blea
Tarn

Elterwater

Skelwith
Bridge

A591
To Grasmere

AMBLESIDE

To
Wrynose
Pass Little Langdale

Tarn Hows

Coniston

B 5285

Hawkshead

WINDERMERE

A591 To Kendal

START

Bowness-on-Windermere

A 593 To Torver

Near Sawrey

FERRY

CONISTON
WATER

WINDERMERE

Tour route with
town or village

Selected other roads

Direction of travel

Steep hill!

*Early morning on the River Brathay, below Elterwater.
If you want to escape the car, there is a delightful
walk along the river bank from Elterwater village
to Skelwith Bridge.*

WINDERMERE TO
SKELWITH BRIDGE

Leaving Windermere on the A591, head
north towards *Ambleside* and *Keswick*.
When you come to a mini-roundabout,
go straight on and continue through
Troutbeck Bridge. After two miles you
will pass *Brockhole*. Like most of the large
houses along this side of the lake, Brockhole was built by a wealthy Lancashire
merchant in the late nineteenth century.
It is now owned by the Lake District
National Park Authority and run as a
visitor centre. It stands right beside the
lake, and has very attractive gardens
which are being restored along the lines
of the original gardens designed by
Thomas Mawson.

Follow the main road past the Low
Wood Hotel, towards the northern end
of the lake. As you enter the outskirts of
Ambleside, take the first left (*Keswick,
Coniston* and *Langdale*), past the landing-

stages and around the head of the lake.
This area is known as Waterhead and
has a classic view across the lake to the
Langdale Pikes. Half a mile later, turn
left (*Coniston, Hawkshead* and *Langdale*),
round the Rothay Manor Hotel and go
left again, over the narrow Rothay bridge.
This is the A593 which takes you through
the tiny hamlet of Clappersgate and past
the turning for Hawkshead, towards
Coniston. If you peer through the trees
on the left you may spot the tower of
Brathay Church.

After a mile or so, turn right at the
Skelwith Bridge Hotel (*Langdale* and
Elterwater) on to the B5343 (ignore the
narrow turning on your extreme right as
you turn off the main road).

SKELWITH BRIDGE TO
LITTLE LANGDALE

This is a narrow country lane, so take
care. You may glimpse Elterwater to your

left, the smallest of the sixteen lakes. It is
only half a mile long and around 48ft
deep and it can freeze in harsh winters.
'Elter' is the Norse word for swan, so this
is literally 'Swan Lake'.

After a mile, the road crosses a cattle
grid and you suddenly come upon a
magnificent view across Elterwater
Common to the Langdales. (There are
one or two lay-bys if you feel a photo
coming on.) The village of Elterwater, a
small collection of Lakeland stone cottages with an attractive village green, is a
short detour to the left. The car-park is
the starting-point for a good walk back
along Great Langdale Beck to the lake,
and the Britannia Inn is a brilliant place to
come for a bar meal on a warm summer
evening (unfortunately everyone else
thinks so too, so get here early).

Continuing along the main road, you
will pass the Langdale Timeshare, and
the cunningly-named Wainwright Inn
(nothing to do with the famous writer).

The road at the head of the valley
seems interminable, but there are plenty
of good views to compensate. Look out
for rock-climbers and fell-walkers – the
New Dungeon Ghyll Hotel is the starting-point for numerous classic Lakeland
walks. The road eventually comes to a
sharp left-hand bend at Stool End
Farm – this is the end of Great Langdale.
Ahead you can see Rossett Ghyll, one
of the major routes on to Bow Fell, and
the craggy 'knuckles' of the attractively-
named Crinkle Crags.

LITTLE LANGDALE TO CONISTON

The road then climbs towards Blea Tarn.
This is an extremely narrow stretch of
road which is quite steep in places (think
of it as good practice for the fourth tour
and Hardknott Pass). Blea Tarn is an
attractive spot; a good place to park and
have a picnic. Just beyond it, the road
drops down a one-in-four hill to enter
Little Langdale, and ahead you will
see Wetherlam and the Old Man of
Coniston.

Two miles further on you come to the junction for Wrynose Pass: continue straight on and over the cattle grid. The road through Little Langdale is very narrow, so it is worth looking out for possible passing places and tooting the horn at the occasional blind bend. Shortly after the Three Shires Inn you arrive at a T-junction. Turn right (signed *Ambleside*) which brings you back to the A593. Go right again (signed *Coniston*). You still need to be careful. Although this is an A road you may still encounter the odd car straddling the white line in a panic (there's something daunting about drystone walls that completely overrides any notion of the road's actual width).

A few hundred yards past Yew Tree Tarn there is a car-park on your left which is handy if you fancy a steep walk to Tarn Hows and wish to avoid the parking charges. A quarter of a mile beyond that, look out for Yew Tree Farm, a classic Lakeland farmhouse with a spinning gallery. As you approach Coniston, watch out for a turning on your left, signed *Hawkshead, Lake* and *Tarn Hows*. (This is a useful shortcut: turn left here and skirt round the edge of the village to join the B5285, then turn left for *Hawkshead* and *Tarn Hows*.)

If you spurn the shortcut, the A593 takes you right into the centre of the village. Then, turn left at the bridge (by the Black Bull Inn) and leave Coniston on the B5285. This route takes you past St Andrew's church – the burial place of John Ruskin – and the Donald Campbell memorial, an unprepossessing green slate seat opposite the car-park. Campbell died on Coniston Water in 1967, during his attempt at the world water-speed record in *Bluebird*.

CONISTON TO TARN HOWS
Heading away from the village, the B5285 takes you past Coniston Water and the turning for Brantwood. After three miles, almost at the top of a hill, you come to an unexpected turning signed *Tarn Hows*. Go left, along the narrow, winding road, turn left again, just by the Summer Hill Country House Hotel, and you'll come to a stunning view of Tarn Hows. There is a National Trust car-park in the woods on your left, where you will be asked for some money. The gentle mile-and-a-half walk round the tarn is easy to follow and highly recommended, though it does get busy.

TARN HOWS TO HAWKSHEAD
Turn right out of the car-park, and go back to the Summer Hill Hotel (if you turn left you will end up again on the A593). Turn left at the hotel and then immediately right (*Hawkshead*). This takes you back to the B5285. Go left again, through Hawkshead Hill and, at the next junction, turn right for *Hawkshead* and *Windermere via ferry*. The road avoids the centre of Hawkshead but a turning right takes you to the main car-park. Vehicles are more or less excluded from the centre, which makes it all the more pleasant to wander around on foot.

Hawkshead is a delightful old town despite the pressure of too many visitors (come back in the evening or early morning to see it at its best). It was an important centre for the wool trade in Norman times, and in the Middle Ages it was a grange, or farm estate, attached to Furness Abbey. William Wordsworth was a pupil at the sixteenth-century grammar school and you can still see the desk where he carved his initials. The school is just opposite the car-park, as you walk towards the centre of Hawkshead. For a good view over the town, continue past the school and up into the grounds of St Michael's church. From here you can walk back down into the square.

HAWKSHEAD TO SAWREY
Fifty yards beyond the turning to the Hawkshead car-park, there is a T-junction. Turn left here (*Sawrey* and *Windermere via ferry*) and drive into the very pleasant countryside familiar to lovers of Beatrix Potter's books. The fields on your right roll down to Esthwaite Water, one of the area's quieter lakes. As you enter Near Sawrey, the car-park for Hill Top is on the right. Beatrix Potter wrote many of her 'little books for children' at Hill Top and, if you have a copy of *The Tale of Pigling Bland*, take a look at the illustrations and try to find the road you've just come along.

Wetherlam from Elterwater, with Lingmoor Fell in the middle distance. Wetherlam lies on the north-east flank of the Old Man of Coniston range, dominating the view from Little Langdale.

Beatrix Potter was born in London in 1865, but spent her holidays in the Lake District. Her first book, *The Tale of Peter Rabbit*, was first published in 1895. She bought Hill Top in 1905; she never lived here full-time but used it as a holiday home. After she married a local solicitor, William Heelis, in 1913, she gave up her writing and devoted herself to sheep farming. When she died, in 1943, she left a total of fifteen farms and 4,000 acres of land including Hill Top, to the National Trust. Her husband's old office in Hawkshead is now the Beatrix Potter Gallery.

Just around the corner from Hill Top is the Tower Bank Arms, another good place for a bar meal (it is a pleasant evening trip via the ferry from Windermere). If you need an excuse, you can always say you've got to call in to see how it compares with the illustration in *Jemima Puddleduck*.

SAWREY TO WINDERMERE

Within seconds of leaving Near Sawrey, you enter the tiny hamlet of Far Sawrey. As the road plummets towards the lake, you get a good view across the water to Bowness. Just as you start to wonder if you will end up in the water, the road veers left, skirting the shore and ending up at Ferry House and the ferry landing-stage.

Depending on the time of day, there may be a queue to board the ferry. You can work out if you have got long to wait from the helpful signs by the road. The trip across only takes five minutes, so it is worth getting out of the car quickly to enjoy the spectacular view north and south along the length of Windermere. Look out for Belle Isle, the tree-covered island just north of the crossing.

Once off the ferry, follow the narrow road to the T-junction and turn left for Bowness. When you reach the mini-roundabout, just past St Martin's church, you could round off the tour with a visit to the Old Laundry Exhibition Centre and The World of Beatrix Potter. To return to Windermere, keep going straight on, through the village centre and back along Lake Road.

This is a route around the heart of the Lake District – the part you will recognize from the picture post-cards. It goes through Ambleside and Hawkshead and into the Lang-dale valley. It is a good way of getting acquainted with the area if you haven't been here before. When touring the southern Lakes, how-ever, all roads seem to lead to Ambleside which can become a desperate bottle-neck in summer. The trick is to make sure you get through early, before all the holiday-makers are on the road. And if you decide to reverse the tour, don't be tempted to cut through Waterhead late in the afternoon; when the roads are busy it can take ages to get out of the junction with the A591, and it becomes quicker to go through the village.

Once you pass Skelwith Bridge and drive into Great Langdale, the pace slows down a little and as you approach Elterwater village, there is a stunning view over the common to the Langdale Pikes. Tarn Hows is also very pretty but can get extremely busy during the summer. This is one to come back to in the evening, when the crowds have gone home. Hill Top, Beatrix Potter's house, is interesting and if you know her stories you can spend hours wandering around Sawrey identifying scenes she painted in her books. I can't think why she decided to buy a house so far from the car-park – most inconsiderate of her!

Finally, the ferry trip across Windermere is an experience in itself. It is remarkably cheap and gives you a completely new perspective on the lake. The staff are very good at packing the maximum number of cars on to the ferry and once underway, there is a good five minutes to get out of the car and enjoy the spectacular views north and south along the length of Windermere. Take the opportunity to look over the side and you'll see that the ferry pulls itself across on steel cables.

Tower Bank Arms, near Sawrey.

TOUR THREE
~
Ullswater and Borrowdale

This tour takes in eight lakes, three mountain passes and some of the most beautiful scenery in England. The route around Borrowdale is particularly spectacular and makes a good mini-tour on its own if you are based in Keswick. Whatever you do, don't miss the short walk to the Bowder Stone to experience one of Lakeland's most famous oddities.

Windermere to Keswick, via Kirkstone Pass – taking in Ullswater, Derwent Water and Borrowdale, and returning via Thirlmere, Grasmere and Rydal.
Distance: 83 miles. Driving time: 5 hours

The scenic village of Grange-in-Borrowdale with its famous bridge crossing the River Derwent.

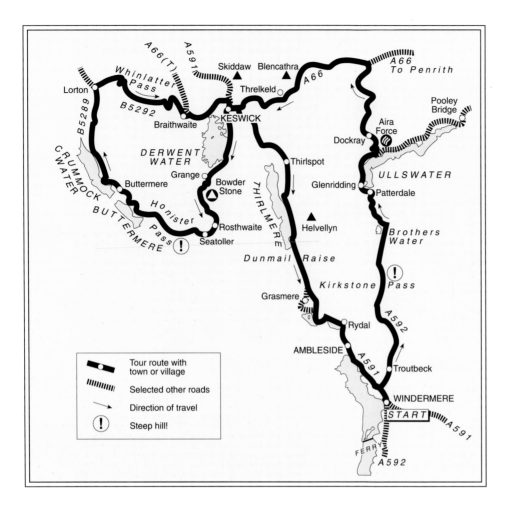

Tour route with town or village

Selected other roads

Direction of travel

(!) Steep hill!

Continuing past the Inn there is a steep drop towards Ullswater, the gradient reaching one-in-five in places. As you start to descend, the large, prominent rock on your left is the Kirk Stone, from which the pass gets its name. Brothers Water comes into sight after a short distance. This is an attractive little tarn, named after two brothers who died here whilst ice-skating in the eighteenth century. Here, you are right in the heart of the mountains, with High Street to the right, Place Fell directly ahead and Fairfield and the Helvellyn range to your left. If you want a longer look at the view, use the National Park car-park at Red Pit, about half a mile into the descent.

The road sweeps down past the Brothers Water Inn and levels out to run alongside the tarn. It is tempting to park here, but better to continue to the far end of the tarn, where there is an excellent car-park. It is a good spot from which to explore the west shore, away from the main road, and perhaps walk a short distance into Dovedale, the pretty, wooded valley below Dove Crag.

Half a mile beyond Brothers Water the view opens up to reveal the surrounding fells. You pass through the small village of Patterdale into Glenridding, and you should see Ullswater and the boat pier on your right. There is a turning on the right for *Glenridding Pier* and the car-park just as you enter the village.

Ullswater is officially a public highway (as are Windermere, Coniston and Derwent Water) although there is a speed limit of ten miles per hour, primarily to deter power boats and water-skiers. The passenger launches are run by the grandly-named Ullswater Navigation and Transit Company. The two steamers are both over 100 years old; *Lady of the Lake* was first launched in 1877 and *Raven* in 1889. As the trading standards board once pointed out, 'steamer' is really a misnomer – they run on diesel.

WINDERMERE TO GLENRIDDING

Leave Windermere along the A591 and follow the road north (*Keswick* and *Ambleside*) until you come to the mini-roundabout. Turn right (*Kirkstone Pass, Ullswater* and *Penrith*) and after a mile you'll pass Holehird, the Leonard Cheshire Home, on your right. This has a very attractive garden which is open to the public. On the left, across the valley, is Troutbeck village. This is really a series of tiny hamlets, clustered around a series of roadside wells. It is worth a detour to visit Townend, a statesman farmer's house dating from 1626. Now owned by the National Trust, it is one of the finest houses open to the public in the Lake District.

To explore the village, there is a turning on the left about two and a half miles along the A592 (*Troutbeck* and *Townend*), just after you cross a bridge, by a very square, stone-built church. If you are keeping to the tour, continue straight on, passing the Queen's Head Hotel with its 'Original Four-Poster Bar' (made from an old four-poster bed). The road begins to climb and you may spot a tall pinnacle on the skyline in front of you; this is Threshwaite Beacon, at the southern end of High Street, the 2,719ft ridge to the east of Kirkstone Pass. At times, it is difficult to see where the road is taking you – within ten minutes of leaving Windermere, you feel you are miles from civilization. The view to your right is very dramatic; the fields falling abruptly away to the floor of the valley.

You eventually reach the summit at the Kirkstone Pass Inn. Congratulations! You're now at 1,489 feet and have climbed one of the Lake District's major mountain passes. It's worth parking opposite the pub and taking in the magnificent view looking back towards Lake Windermere.

GLENRIDDING TO KESWICK

As you leave the village and follow the lake shore, there are a number of lay-bys which give you the chance to do some exploring on foot. Ullswater is the second longest lake in England (Windermere is ten and a half miles long and Ullswater seven and a half) and many would say it is the most beautiful. The landscape changes from drama and grandeur at the head of the lake, to the gentle, rolling scenery around its foot, or lower end, at Pooley Bridge. This is superb walking country, particularly along the south-east shore where there is no road. The best way to see it is to catch a steamer to Howtown and walk back to Glenridding.

Three miles out of the village, turn left on to the A5091, signed *Dockray, Matterdale, Troutbeck* and *Keswick*. (If you want to make a detour to the car-park and café at Aira Force, continue past this turning and carry on 100yds or so further along the A592. The car-park is owned by the National Trust and there is a parking charge.) Once on the A5091 the passengers get all the best views, looking back towards Ullswater, Place Fell and High Street. After half a mile, look out for a car-park on the right – this one is free and gives a much shorter downhill walk to Aira Force. This 70ft cascade is probably the most famous waterfall in the District. 'Force,' by the way, is the local name for waterfall.

The road climbs on to Matterdale Common, through Dockray village and past the isolated lump of Great Mell Fell. From the common there is an excellent view of Blencathra, one of Lakeland's most attractive fells. The road takes you through another Troutbeck and then to a junction with the A66. Turn left (signed *Keswick*) and look out for the minuscule weather station on your left as you make the turning. The A66 by-passes Keswick, so as you approach the town take the turning right, signed *Keswick* and *Windermere*. This takes you under the A66 and into the outskirts. At the next T-junction, turn right (*Town Centre* and *Borrowdale*, B5289). Not the most glamorous route into Keswick but it avoids a lot of hazards – and you come back to the town centre at

the end of the route.

You pass the River Greta and a large, open park on your right. Once round the corner there's a large pay-and-display car-park on your left, very handy for the town centre (so it is often full). Just off the car-park is the Cars of the Stars Museum, which features cars used in major films and television series. The road skirts Market Place and then abruptly turns away from the centre. A couple of hundred yards beyond, take the turning left, signed *Town Centre* and *Borrowdale*, along Heads Road. Keep bearing left, past another car-park and at the mini-roundabout go straight across (*Borrowdale*). At the next roundabout, go right. You are now entering Borrowdale and have left behind the traffic and confusion of Keswick. Phew!

KESWICK TO BUTTERMERE

Look down the valley and you can see where the crags on either side of the road seem to meet ahead of you. The eighteenth-century guide-book writers named these the Jaws of Borrowdale. The scenery is very rough and majestic; high crags rising above the wooded valley bottom. It is a favourite playground for rock-climbers, a breed whose collective dress sense is anything but conservative, so you should have no trouble spotting them on the crags.

As you drive alongside Derwent Water there are National Trust car-parks dotted along the road. Unfortunately, the Trust has begun to charge for parking, but at least the charge is kept low and you can use the ticket in any other Trust car-park on the same day. The road passes the foot of Derwent Water and the Lodore Swiss Hotel and then follows the River Derwent. As you pass the turning for Grange-in-Borrowdale, look out for the double-arched

bridge over the river.

Half a mile beyond Grange there's a sign and a car-park on your left for the *Bowder Stone*, one of the Lake District's most impressive landmarks, and it's well worth the short walk to explore it. There is a ladder on one side and you can climb to the top. If you've got strong nerves, there is a gap underneath the boulder, where you can reach through and shake hands with someone on the other side.

As you drive past the Bowder Stone, look at the conical fell ahead of you. This is Castle Crag, so named because an Iron Age fort once commanded the valley from this position. The road then brings you to the tiny village of Rosthwaite. If you fancy a stop, there is a car-park as you enter the village just up the little lane on the right. The local ice-creams from the post office are brilliant, but work up an appetite first; from the car-park walk up

the lane and go and explore the banks of the Derwent.

From Rosthwaite the road takes you into the tiny hamlet of Seatoller. On your right is an information centre, known as the National Park Seatoller Barn Dale Head Base for short, which holds various craft-oriented events over the summer. Once beyond the village, you start to climb Honister Pass. Compared to some, this is a relatively easy pass, reaching 1,176ft at the summit. The steep bits are good practice for the fourth tour. The main impediment to progress is an appallingly rough road surface – during hot summers all the tarmac seems to migrate to the foot of the pass.

When you reach the top, there is a car-park next to Honister Quarry, beside the old buildings for the Buttermere and Westmorland Green Slate Company. The road descends an abrupt one-in-four gradient towards Buttermere, and

Above: The southern end of Ullswater, looking across to Glenridding village and St Sunday Crag.
Opposite: Aira Force, the area's best-known waterfall, with a splendid walk alongside the wooded ravine.

the short stretch immediately past the mine buildings is particularly difficult in wet or icy conditions.

Watch out for suicidal sheep as you bowl along the valley bottom; they like nothing better than to wait until you've drawn almost alongside them and then they leap off the bank into the road.

You will encounter two main breeds of sheep in the Lake District: Herdwick and Swaledale. Herdwicks have white faces and black wool, which gets lighter with age. Only the males have horns. They are a very tough breed, ideally adapted to the harsh conditions on the fells. Swaledales are shorter, with dark faces and lighter-coloured wool, and both sexes have horns.

BUTTERMERE TO LORTON

At Gatesgarth Farm you have reached the head of Buttermere Lake. The small car-park by the farm is unofficial and expensive. Unfortunately, the roadside from here doesn't offer much alternative as there are double yellow lines on both sides. This gives you an idea of how popular it can get in summer. By far the best place to park is in Buttermere village. Buttermere ('the lake in the dairy pastures') is a very pretty little lake with an easy circular walk around it, starting from the village. On the east side, hidden from the road, the footpath goes through a short tunnel, blasted through rock.

As you follow the road, you're surrounded by fells on all sides – Goat Crag and Robinson above you on the right, the long ridge of Red Pike on the far side and Haystacks and Fleetwith Pike at the head of the lake. And as you enter Buttermere village, past the turning for

Keswick and *Newlands*, look out for the turning left by the Bridge Hotel. This takes you down to a car-park beside the river. There is another larger car-park just as you leave the village.

The other pub in Buttermere is the Fish Hotel (originally the Fish Inn), the scene of a famous nineteenth-century scandal. A gentleman posing as the Honourable Colonel Alexander Augustus Hope, MP, stayed here in 1802 and eloped to Gretna Green with Mary Robinson, the landlord's daughter. Unfortunately for Mary, on their return to Buttermere, Hope was unmasked as James Hatfield, a notorious bigamist and swindler. He was obviously a skilled con man for, in the midst of all the fuss, he persuaded the local constable to let him go fishing on the lake. They caught up with him again in Wales, two months later. Such were the outcry and public sympathy for Mary that he was hanged at

Carlisle in 1803.

Coleridge, who was living at the time in Greta Hall at Keswick, wrote about the affair in the London *Morning Post*. Once playwrights got hold of the story, it ran and ran for over 100 years. In 1987 there was a revival of interest when Melvyn Bragg – another native Cumbrian – published his novel, *The Maid of Buttermere*. Mary Robinson eventually married a farmer called Harrison and is buried in Caldbeck churchyard, which is visited in the first tour.

Once through a small wood, you drive alongside Crummock Water. Long and winding, this lake has a remote feel more akin to a Scottish loch. In fact, its name is Celtic, meaning 'curved lake'. Beyond Crummock Water, you're into open countryside, with rolling hills ahead and fells rising to Hopegill Head on your right. A mile and a half beyond the lake, you come to a T-junction. Go right, towards *Scale Hill* and *Lorton*.

This valley is Lorton Vale, very pretty and little explored by the majority of tourists. As you enter the village of Low Lorton, take the turning right (*Keswick*), and you come to High Lorton. Once through this village, turn right (*Braithwaite* and *Keswick*) and, at the T-junction, turn right again and on to Whinlatter Pass.

LORTON TO KESWICK

Whinlatter is the easiest Lakeland pass; a long, wide road which climbs through Thornthwaite Forest, alongside the Lorton Fells. After three and a half miles, you pass the Forestry Commission Visitor Centre at Whinlatter. As you descend, past the Cottage in the Wood hotel and restaurant, you start to get a good view of Keswick and the foot of Bassenthwaite Lake. The road then brings you down to Braithwaite village. Carry on straight through and out at the T-junction. Turn right on to the A66, back towards Keswick.

If you only meandered round the outskirts of Keswick earlier in the tour, this time you may wish to drive into the centre to park and explore. A mile along the A66, you'll come to the turning for *Keswick* and this takes you down the B5289, through the area known as Crosthwaite. This is the old part of Keswick. The church is St Kentigern's (also called St Mungo's) and is the burial place of Hugh Walpole, author of the *Herries Chronicles*. He lived for a time in a house on the west side of Derwent Water and based his *Herries* novels in the area. Inside the church there is a bust of the poet Robert Southey, paid for by the Brazilian government after he wrote the first official history of their country (without actually visiting it).

Follow the signs for *Windermere* as they lead you through Keswick and out on to the A591. A mile or so out of town, look out for a narrow turning on your left, signed *Castlerigg Stone Circle*, and turn

off here if you wish to visit the spectacular prehistoric site described in the first tour.

KESWICK TO GRASMERE

Continue along the main road and as you drop downhill there is a magnificent view of St John's in the Vale. The distinctive crag on your left is Castle Rock of Triermain, the inspiration for Sir Walter Scott's novel *The Bridal of Triermain*. As soon as you come off the dual carriageway, take the turning to the right on to a minor road, signed *Public road round lake*. This takes you round the quieter, western shore of Thirlmere.

Originally there were two smaller lakes here, Brackmere and Leatheswater, but in 1879 they were bought by Manchester Corporation Water Works and a dam was built to flood the valley. Access to the lake shore has only been possible in recent years, since the Victorian filter works were upgraded. You will come across several car-parks along this narrow road. In hot weather, Thirlmere suffers from drought faster than any of the other lakes, but if the lake is full, the views south to Dunmail Raise can be wonderful.

Rejoin the A591 and turn right up

Dunmail Raise. Dunmail was the last king of the Cumbrians and according to local legend he is buried under the pile of stones in the middle of the dual carriageway, having been killed on this spot during battle with King Edmund of England in AD 945. It is more likely, however, that he died during a pilgrimage to Rome, several years later.

Once over the summit, you are greeted by the magnificent view of the vale of Grasmere. Loughrigg Terrace is directly ahead of you, on the far side of the lake. Follow the fell round to the right and you come to Silver How. The fell directly to your right is Helm Crag, also known as The Lion and The Lamb – locals maintain you can see the shapes of these two beasts in the rocks on the summit. Only slightly less fanciful was one seventeenth-century writer who maintained that it was an extinct volcano.

The road now drops into Grasmere and to get to the village centre, you have to make a detour off the main road. Turn right opposite the Swan Hotel and the road takes you through the centre and rejoins the A591 opposite the turning for *Dove Cottage* at Town End. Grasmere is to many people the classic Lakeland village, tucked away beside a lake, surrounded by fells. It was Wordsworth who really made the place famous. He lived at Dove Cottage from 1799 until 1808, during the time when he was producing most of his best poetry. His sister Dorothy chronicled their daily lives in her diary. The house is much as it was in Wordsworth's day and the Dove Cottage Trust has managed to reclaim most of his original furniture. If you only have time to visit one Wordsworth property, this is definitely the best. Try and get here early, and see if you can bag one of the guides for yourself.

GRASMERE TO WINDERMERE

The road runs alongside the lake, giving you a good view of its small island. The building you can glimpse in the trees is an old barn. Farmers used to graze sheep on the island, rowing them over in flat-bottomed boats. As you leave the lake, you come to White Moss Common car-

park (and probably an ice-cream van). If you park here and walk across the road, you can follow the River Rothay upstream to Grasmere Lake.

The road brings you alongside Rydal Water and past Nab Cottage. This once belonged to another notable literary figure, Thomas De Quincey, who came to Grasmere in 1807 to visit his great hero, Wordsworth. In fact, this was his third attempt as his nerve had failed him on the previous occasions. When he finally got to Dove Cottage, he stayed several months and eventually took on the tenancy when Wordsworth and his family moved to Allan Bank. De Quincey wrote his notorious *Confessions of an English Opium Eater* at Dove Cottage.

Whilst living at Grasmere, De Quincey began to court Margaret Simpson, who lived at Nab Cottage (or as it was then, Nab Farm). Wordsworth – who had become a bit of a snob – disapproved and kept writing to De Quincey's mother, warning her about the liaison. De Quincey later married Margaret and got his revenge on Wordsworth and his circle in a delightfully catty book called *Recollections of the Lakes and the Lake Poets*. He eventually bought Nab Farm from Margaret's father in 1829, but kept on the lease to Dove Cottage, just to store his books.

Entering Rydal there is a turning on the left for *Rydal Mount*. Wordsworth lived here until his death in 1850. The house has a lovely view along the valley to the head of Windermere. Just past this turning there is a small bridge on your right. This is Pelter Bridge, named after the first man to drive a horse and cart across it when it was opened. If you drive across and turn right again you'll come to a small car-park from which you can walk to Rydal Water.

From Rydal follow the main road south to Ambleside. Once through Ambleside, continue south along the main road and back to Windermere.

This is a very pretty drive which takes you over two of the Lakeland passes – Kirkstone and Honister. They're nowhere near as steep and tortuous as Hardknott or Wrynose (which feature in Tour Four) so you can regard them as practice runs. The views on this route are breathtaking, but don't despair if the weather is bad; when the clouds come down and the rain sets in, although you lose the long view along Ullswater from Kirkstone Pass, the section around Borrowdale valley is still good. The valley walls are so steep and so close to the road that you have to be driving through thick mist before you lose sight of them.

If you're staying in the north Lakes, Borrowdale makes an excellent short tour in its own right. When you explore the valley, don't miss the Bowder Stone. This 36ft high, 1,900 ton boulder was left here by the glaciers during the last Ice Age. It's one of the Lake District's natural wonders and shouldn't be missed. My son, Elliot, loved it. It seems to be balanced on one edge and as you walk under the sides, it's hard to believe that it won't topple over at any moment.

Finally, when you come back through Keswick, the Cars of the Stars Museum is highly recommended. It features the actual vehicles used in movies and television, including two of the James Bond cars, Emma Peel's Lotus Elan from the *Avengers*, Chitty-Chitty Bang-Bang, a Batmobile from the 1960s television series, and a life-size version of Lady Penelope's pink Rolls Royce from *Thunderbirds*, as well as cars which have appeared in *M.A.S.H.*, *The Prisoner* and *All Creatures Great and Small*. It is a private collection which was only recently opened to the public. The museum's latest acquisition is the DeLorean from *Back to the Future*.

If you need to get back in a hurry at the end of the tour, you can always keep to the A591, avoiding the detour along the west side of Thirlmere.

The Bowder Stone, Borrowdale.

TOUR FOUR
~
The Western Lakes

The west coast of Cumbria contains some
of the wildest and least explored
countryside in the Lake District. Few
visitors from the central Lakes ever seem
to get out this way, perhaps deterred by
the long trek. This is a good route to
escape the crowds on a bank holiday
Monday and includes England's deepest
lake, steepest pass and biggest liar.

From Ambleside, over Hardknott and Wrynose Pass to
Eskdale and Ravenglass, with a chance to explore
Wastwater, Ennerdale, Loweswater and Crummock
Water, and returning via Buttermere, the Newlands
Valley, Keswick and Grasmere.
Distance: 104 miles. Driving time: 5–6 hours

Helvellyn, seen through the morning mist rising from Thirlmere.
The lake is a reservoir, and was only recently opened up to the public.

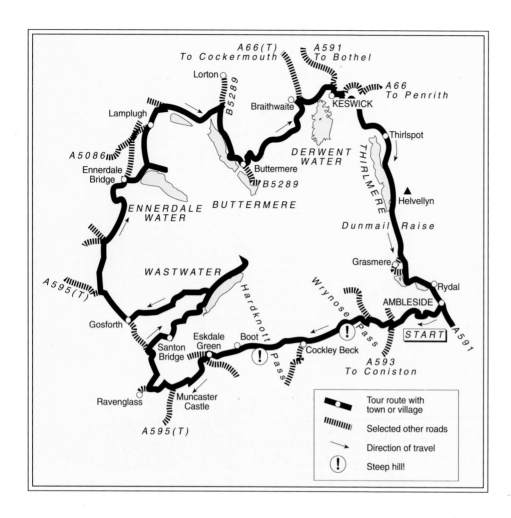

The road through Little Langdale is incredibly narrow in places and the dry-stone walls can hinder visibility, so keep your eyes open for likely passing places.

AMBLESIDE TO LITTLE LANGDALE

Leave Ambleside along the A591, as if heading to Windermere, and turn right at the petrol station (*Coniston, Hawkshead* and *Langdale*). At the T-junction, turn left, continuing to follow the signs for *Coniston* and *Hawkshead*. Take the next right, around the Rothay Manor Hotel and left over Rothay Bridge. Follow the A593 through Clappersgate and towards Coniston. You then pass Skelwith Bridge and the Kirkstone Slate Gallery. You can park here and there is a good walk along the river to Skelwith Force. There is also a good tea-shop in the slate gallery.

A mile past Skelwith Bridge take the turning on the right, signed *Wrynose, Elterwater* and *The Langdales*. This takes you into Little Langdale and onto a very narrow lane, so watch out for oncoming traffic in the middle of the road. After a mile or so, there is a magnificent view of Wetherlam on your left, and directly ahead you should be able to make out the road ascending Wrynose Pass.

WRYNOSE AND HARDKNOTT

About a mile past the Three Shires Inn and Little Langdale Tarn, take the turning on the left for *Wrynose Pass*. The road immediately becomes even narrower. After about a third of a mile, prepare to breathe in to squeeze your car through the gap by Fell Foot Farm. (Watch out for farm dogs on the road.)

Wrynose is one of the most famous mountain passes in Britain, though Hardknott is steeper. It's fairly straightforward as long as you take it steady and keep your eye on potential passing places. In theory, the car climbing has right of way, but not everyone seems to know this. Passengers looking back will get a good view of Little Langdale Tarn and the head of Lake Windermere; drivers will probably find all their attention concentrated on the way the ground drops steeply to the left-hand side of the road. There's a parking place at the

If you are planning a trip round the Lakes in the middle of spring, don't forget your thermal underwear and the snow chains – these are winter conditions on Hardknott Pass in May. . . .

summit, but there are better views from the top of Hardknott, so press on . . .

Just beyond the summit of Wrynose there is a stone column. This is the Three Shires Stone, marking the meeting point of the old county boundaries of Lancashire, Westmorland and Cumberland. The road descends steeply to Wrynose Bottom and you have a chance to get your breath back before tackling Hardknott Pass. If you want to frighten your passengers, point out the road up Hardknott, just to the left of the ravine directly ahead.

After a mile and a half of fairly flat driving you come to a junction at Cockley Beck Farm. Go right, over a bridge and through the farm gate on the other side. The gate will probably be closed, so a passenger will have to do the honours. (Occasionally, in summer, entrepreneurial schoolchildren hang about at the gate, offering to open it for a fee.) At this point you pass an encouraging road sign – *Steep Hill, 30% (1-in-3).* Don't be put off – you encounter the most difficult part almost immediately. As you approach a road bridge, remind yourself where you put first gear; this bit is a steep, hairpin bend and the road surface is rough, just to add to the fun. If you can do this, you're ready for anything later on (although it does lack the psychological impact of some of the subsequent stretches).

You gain height rapidly, via a number of hairpin bends and severe palpitations. Look out for cars coming down. (You might also like to keep an eye on the temperature gauge, especially on hot, summer days, and stop for a while if necessary. It's embarrassing to break down because your engine has overheated.) It's only half a mile to the top. Once you've reached the summit, park and have a good look at the view (besides, you need to gather your strength for the next bit). As you descend, there's a superb view along the Eskdale valley to

the sea. Once again, the road has hairpin bends and falls away at the sides. Don't forget to give way to anyone coming up.

There is a wonderful Roman fort on the dramatic mountain spur, below the summit of Hardknott. A good way to find it is to look for the cars or Mountain Goat mini-bus in the lay-by, half-way down. It's also at about this point that you'll smell burning brakes if you haven't engaged a low enough gear for the descent.

Although it is now known as Hardknott Fort, the Romans called it Mediobogdum and it stood guard over the road from Galava (Waterhead, at Ambleside) to Glannaventa (Ravenglass). It was occupied during the second century AD by the Fourth Cohort of Dalmations, during the rule of Emperor Hadrian, and probably abandoned some time in the third century. The fort has a superb view and on a clear

day you can look out to the Isle of Man.

ESKDALE AND RAVENGLASS

The road descends into a very green, lush valley, one of the prettiest and least spoilt in the Lake District. There are a number of superb, low-level walks beside the River Esk. One of the best starts from St Catherine's church, which lies at the end of a narrow lane opposite the turning for Boot and the Brook House hotel and restaurant. A couple of hundred yards beyond the turning is Dalegarth station, the terminus for the Ravenglass and Eskdale Railway.

After a further two miles, you arrive at a T-junction, just opposite the King George IV pub. Turn left (*Ulpha* and *Broughton*) and half a mile beyond that, look out for a turning to the right. This is not signed and is a very narrow road. Turn right here and the road takes you through the trees, heading towards Muncaster Fell. If you look carefully, you will see Muncaster Castle, the home of the Pennington family since the thirteenth century. It has a lovely setting overlooking the estuary. You then meet the A595. Turn right (*Workington, Ravenglass* and *Muncaster Castle*) and as you climb the hill there is a good view to the central Lakeland fells and the Scafell range on your right.

The public entrance for Muncaster Castle is a mile along the main road, just as you're beginning to descend towards the coast. Less than a mile later, the road goes round a broad right-hand bend and you turn left for *Ravenglass*. The road into the village is a dead-end, taking you straight into the car-park. It's worth stopping here and exploring the village. The main street is unusual – it runs straight down on to the beach (there's a large metal flood-gate at the end). You can stand here and look out over the estuary, past the moored yachts (or grounded yachts, depending on the state of the tide) to Eskmeal Dunes.

In Roman times, this was the second largest port in Britain, the only natural harbour between the Dee and the Solway. It is difficult to believe, looking at this view, that it was active as a port till the end of the eighteenth century, when the harbour began to silt up. Eskmeal Dunes is a coastal nature reserve, home of a large breeding colony of black-headed gulls.

Across the railway line from the car-park is the main station for the Ravenglass and Eskdale Railway where there's also a small museum. Walk out of the car-park and follow the road back out of the village, and after 600yds you come to a lane on your right. This is a bridle-way which leads you to Walls Castle, the old Roman bath house to the fort of Glannaventa. It is still largely intact with walls of over twelve ft high in places and the highest standing walls of any Roman ruin in the north of England. The rest of the Roman fort is now dispersed among the brickwork of local houses. The final remains were destroyed by Victorian workmen when the construction of the main railway was underway.

RAVENGLASS TO WAST WATER

From Ravenglass, go back to the A595 and turn left (*Workington*). On the left, you can see the cooling towers of Sellafield and one of the country's greatest collections of electricity pylons. After a mile, you pass Muncaster Mill on your right and then, a mile and a half beyond that, just as you come within sight of Holmrook and the petrol station, turn right on to a minor road, signed *Santon Bridge* and *Eskdale Green*. As you follow this narrow lane along a lovely avenue of maples, look out for glimpses of Wasdale screes ahead of you. After about three miles, you come to a T-junction; go left (*Wasdale, Gosforth* and *Whitehaven*). This takes you into Santon Bridge.

The Santon Bridge Inn is the home of the Greatest Liar in the World competition. This eccentric Cumbrian activity is held each year in honour of Will Ritson, the original Great Liar and landlord of the Wasdale Head Inn. He used to boast that Wasdale contained the deepest lake, highest mountain and biggest liar in England. The competition attracts entries from all over the county, but professionals – such as politicians, lawyers and journalists – are barred from entry.

Just before the bridge, turn right (*Wasdale*) and a narrow, hedge-lined road takes you back towards the fells. At the next bridge, turn right (*Wasdale Head*), on to another narrow road. At the next T-junction, turn right again and this takes you to the shores of Wast Water. This is the Lake District's deepest lake. The spectacular 2,000ft high screes on the far shore run right to the bed of the lake, 258ft below the surface. On a calm, still day, they can be reflected in the lake and seem to go down forever.

As you drive along the shore, the view ahead – Great Gable, flanked by Kirk Fell (on the left) and Lingmell – may look familiar; it is the emblem for the Lake District National Park. Turn right at the next junction (where a pleasant sign indicates *Greendale*) and you gradually approach the head of the valley. The dramatic fell ahead of you is Yewbarrow and to the right you can see Scafell Pike.

Looking along Wast Water towards Wasdale Head, with Great Gable flanked by Kirk Fell (on the left) and Lingmell – this view is used as the logo for the Lake District National Park.

You can park just before the Wasdale Head Inn. It is worth exploring the footpath which leads to the tiny church of St Olaf's. Look at the amazing drystone walls in the fields at the head of the valley – it is hard to imagine how some of them keep standing.

Drystone walls are a major feature of the Lakes. They are built without any mortar or cement – think of that when you see them heading straight up an apparently perpendicular fell. The oldest wall in the area was built by the Cistercian monks of Furness Abbey and its remains lie just below Hardknott. Most Lakeland walls were built to enclose common land, following the Enclosure Act of 1801, although the ones at Wasdale Head serve mainly to clear the fields of rubble. If you fancy having a go at building one (and it is more fiendish than it looks) there is a practice wall and frequent demonstrations at Brockhole, the National Park Visitor Centre. If you're really keen, the Park organizes work parties and you can go out for a day and do some wall repairs.

WASTWATER TO ENNERDALE

Once you've finished admiring the walls, follow the road back to the Greendale sign and go right (*Gosforth*). This winding road brings you into the village of Gosforth. There's a car-park in the centre, just opposite the Lakeland Habit outdoor shop (which has a wonderful café upstairs). Walk back along the road to St Mary's church and look for the amazing eleventh-century sandstone cross. It's one of the finest in Britain and covered in intricate carvings. From Gosforth, keep following the road north, past Gosforth Pottery and back to the A595. Turn right on to a fast, wide road with pleasant rural scenery – from here you're hard pressed to spot the Lakeland fells.

After three miles, turn right on to a minor road just by the church at Calder Bridge. There is no sign, so take care not

half a mile. Straight ahead you can see Grasmoor, with the distinctive, conical shape of Mellbreak on the right (the lower conical fell alongside it is Low Bank). As you approach Crummock Water, keep straight on – ignoring the turning for *Loweswater* – and cross the River Cocker. Just past the bridge is the Scale Hill Hotel. Half a mile beyond that turn right for *Buttermere* and *Crummock Water*.

The road runs alongside Crummock Water, giving a good view across the lake to Mellbreak and Ling Crags. Eventually you come into Buttermere village. Just past the Bridge Hotel and Syke Farm, turn left by the church (*Keswick*). The road now climbs towards Newlands Pass.

BUTTERMERE TO KESWICK

Newlands is an impressive sight. For once, the drive along the distinctive V-shaped river valley is sufficiently gentle for the driver to have the opportunity to look at the view. On your right is one of the most entertainingly named fells in the Lakes – High Snockrigg. After a mile and a quarter, you arrive at Newlands Hause, the 1,100ft high summit. You can park here and explore Mass Force, the waterfall by the road. There are excellent views ahead to Blencathra and Keswick. To the right are Maiden Moor and Cat Bells.

The descent is superb, with views down the valley to Robinson and Hindscarth. Newlands is the prettiest of the Lakeland passes and what it lacks in drama it makes up for in charm. That is until you suddenly come to a purple wooden house called Rigg Beck, which, if nothing else, serves as a useful landmark. Go right here (*Newlands Church* and *Littletown*), past the sign for Newlands Church and go over a little bridge before bearing left through the aptly-named Littletown. When you come to a T-junction, turn right (*Portinscale* and *Grange*) and, at the next, go left. This takes you past Lingholm Gardens and

to miss it. Half a mile further on, take the turning on the left, for *Ennerdale Bridge*. This climbs on to a windswept moor, heading back towards the fells. As you come off Kinniside Common, you can see Ennerdale Water on your right. Take the next turning to the right (*Ennerdale Bridge*), and half a mile beyond that, right again (*Ennerdale Water* and *Crossfell*). Follow the road, ignoring the turnings for Ennerdale Lake (which take you to the foot of the lake) and after three and a quarter miles you arrive at Bowness Knott car-park.

You can drive alongside every lake in the Lake District apart from Ennerdale Water. There is a Forestry Commission road to the head of the lake, but they are apt to get a bit cross if you use it. Park at Bowness Knott and climb the slight hill to look down at the lake. Just below are – in our opinion – the two best sited picnic tables in the Lake

District. The rocky point on the far shore is Angler's Crag.

ENNERDALE TO BUTTERMERE

From Bowness Knott, follow the road for two miles, back to the crossroads and turn right (*Lamplugh*). Follow the narrow, winding road to the top of the moor, where you're rewarded by a superb view of the Solway Firth and the Galloway Hills. This road follows the boundary of the National Park for a while. At the next T-junction, turn right (*Loweswater* and *Buttermere*) into Lamplugh. At the turning for *Loweswater* and *Buttermere* go right again. This is a pleasant stretch of road, and as you pass the turning for Mockerkin, you'll find that you're at the improbably named Fangs Brow. Once you have got over that you're heading back into the Lakes and down into a lovely wooded valley beside Loweswater.

The road runs along beside the lake for

into Portinscale. Follow the main road (*Keswick* and *Cockermouth*) and at the A66, turn right for Keswick.

You have a choice as you approach Keswick: if you need a tea and a stop, turn right into the town centre; if you feel like getting home, continue straight past until you come to a roundabout. Go straight across (*Motorway* and *Windermere*). After a mile and a half, a slip-road left takes you on to the A591 for Windermere. It then sweeps under the A66 and into the outskirts of Keswick. After half a mile, turn left at the T-junction (*Windermere, A591*) and the road climbs away from Keswick.

KESWICK TO AMBLESIDE

If you have already done the third tour, you'll be an expert on the road back to Ambleside and Windermere. This time, however, once you come off the dual carriageway, keep on the A591 and continue along the east shore of Thirlmere. About four and a half miles along the lake, you get a glimpse of the old Victorian pumping station on your right. A mile and a half beyond that is Swirls, a car-park with some good walks, particularly back through the woods on the left of the road.

As you get back into Ambleside, look out for the Bridge House, on your right, just past the first car-park. This is one of the most famous buildings in the Lake District and probably the most photographed for postcards. It stands over Stock Beck, giving rise to the local legend that it was built by a wily Scotsman to avoid Land Tax. In fact it used to be the apple store for Ambleside Hall, in the days when this part of Ambleside was thickly wooded. It is now a National Trust information centre, but in the past has been a weaver's shop, a family home, a cobbler's and a tiny café.

If you walk across the road and follow the beck upstream, you pass the last remaining water-wheel, from one of Ambleside's old mills. Continue left, up the back lane and you come to a wooded area and a walk to Stock Ghyll Force, a very pretty waterfall much loved by the early Victorian sightseers.

At 104 miles, this is the longest route in the book and features some of the most spectacular scenery. To have time to explore it fully, try to set out early. There is no need to rush to get round everything – once you get to Keswick, the A591 back to Windermere is very direct and can be quite quick in late afternoon.

If you haven't done it before, the drive over Wrynose and Hardknott is an experience not to be missed. Don't be put off by the steep gradients and the hairpin bends. Take them at a steady pace and remember the two golden rules: check your car before you set out (oil and coolant especially) and use the passing places to give way to cars driving uphill.

Problems only occur if you meet someone who insists on hogging the middle of the road. This happened to me once on Hardknott Pass. Pulling over, I caught a rock with the wall of a tyre. I soon realized I had a puncture and pulled over to change the wheel. In these circumstances, it's always important to get the damaged tyre repaired as soon as you can, and so I called into the garage at Eskdale Green. It was a Sunday lunch time, but someone got the engineer out of the pub and he fixed the tyre right away. He couldn't have been more helpful.

Once over Hardknott, you're in the lovely valley of Eskdale. Don't miss the Ravenglass and Eskdale Railway. The line was built in 1875 to transport haematite from the iron mines at Boot. Known locally as 'La'al Ratty', it is more than just a tourist attraction, running all winter to carry commuters down the valley to catch the main west-coast line. If you have time, you can park at Dalegarth Station, take a steam train to Ravenglass, explore the village and Walls Castle, then catch the train back to the car. During the summer, services in both directions are pretty frequent and it is a splendid trip.

La'al Ratty, Eskdale.

TOUR FIVE
~
The Duddon Valley

This is a tour along narrow, wooded

lanes, past dark, mysterious lakes, through

a quiet, isolated valley and over a high

mountain pass . . . the ancient industrial

heartland of the Lake District. It also gives

you the opportunity to visit the house with

the best view in England.

Ambleside to Hall Dunnerdale, via Consiton Water,
Torver, Broughton-in-Furness and Ulpha, returning over
Wrynose Pass.
Distance: 50 miles. Driving time: 3½–4 hours

*The River Duddon above Birks Bridge at the head of
Dunnerdale looking north towards the Ulpha Fells.*

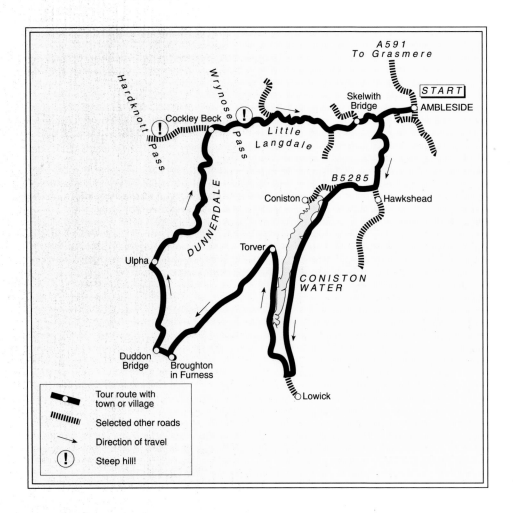

Ignore the temptation of turnings to Tarn Hows (sometimes referred to as 'The Tarns').

A mile beyond Hawkshead Hill, there is a turning to the left, just as the main road bears round to the right. Take this turning (signed *East of Lake*), effectively going straight off the main road. Look out for the water pump and trough in the wall. This is a narrow, pretty lane which slowly weaves its way downhill through coppice woodland. Just past Atkinson Ground there is an unexpected and delightful view across the floor of the valley to the head of Coniston Water and Coniston village.

At the Y-junction turn left on to another minor road (*Newby Bridge* and *East of Lake*). As it climbs there is an even better view of the village set against the spectacular backdrop of the Old Man of Coniston. Using the village as a sight, look straight into the valley behind (known locally as Coppermines Valley); the tall peak to the left is the Old Man, and to the right of the valley are Swirl How and then Wetherlam. The cluster of buildings and boats on the far shore is Coniston Boating Centre.

This view keeps reappearing, but it's worth being patient because the best viewpoint of all is at Brantwood, John Ruskin's home. The house is about a mile down the road. Use the car-park, just beyond the entrance, and walk back up to the house.

John Ruskin, the writer, art critic and philosopher, bought the house in 1871, sight unseen, for £1,500. When he got here he found 'a mere shed of rotten timbers and loose stone' but also discovered one of the finest views in England. He transformed it into a beautiful home and lived here until his death in 1900. The house is open to the public – in line with Ruskin's own wishes. Make sure you take in the view from the little turret window in the main bedroom. The house also contains some fine paintings by

AMBLESIDE TO BRANTWOOD

From the centre of Ambleside, head south along the one-way system towards Windermere. Turn right, opposite the petrol station (*Coniston, Hawkshead* and *Langdale*). Go left at the bottom of the hill and, half a mile farther on, take the first right (*Coniston, Hawkshead* and *Langdale*). This takes you round the Rothay Manor Hotel. Go left over Rothay Bridge.

At Clappersgate, take the first turning on the left (*B5286 Hawkshead*). This takes you over the River Brathay. This is a very pleasant stretch of tree-lined river bank. Just over the bridge, there is a short lay-by on your right if you want to stop.

The road meanders through woods and fields, and a mile or so after crossing the Brathay look out for a sign for *Coniston, Tarn Hows* and *The Drunken Duck* on your right. Continue past the turning, but bear it in mind for future

reference; the Drunken Duck does excellent bar meals and is one of the most popular pubs in the area. It is in a lovely, isolated setting and is a good place to head for on a warm summer evening. As you wander along the B-road you may meet the occasional lorry, so be prepared to pull into the side and shuffle past. Oncoming cars, too, sometimes seem to be magnetically drawn to the centre of the road.

Half a mile beyond the hamlet of Outgate, the hedges and walls at the roadside give way to lines of vertical slates. These are called shard stones and are peculiar to the Hawkshead and Coniston areas. After another half-mile you cross a little bridge and turn right (*Tarn Hows, Coniston* and *Gondola Steamboat Pier*) on to the B5285, which climbs steeply.

Shortly after the hamlet of Hawkshead Hill there is a view of Coniston Old Man.

Turner, of whom he was an energetic champion.

It is worth calling in at the Jumping Jenny tea-room, in the old stable block, where there is also a small craft gallery upstairs. The tea-room takes its name from Ruskin's boat.

BRANTWOOD TO LOWICK

Beyond Brantwood the woods close in again and you lose the view. Half a mile from Brantwood, there is a car-park with access to the lake. One of the beauties of this meandering, wooded road is the number of car-parks; there are five, all free and all just where you want them when the road meets the shore.

The best car-park is saved until last, just over two and a half miles from Brantwood, at Parkamoor. This is a large parking area with several picnic tables dotted about amongst the trees. On the shore is a wooden jetty for the Gondola steam launch. Try to time your arrival to coincide with the launch (timetable from any tourist or National Trust information centre), and make sure you have your camera. The Gondola is an original nineteenth-century steam launch, a splendid, wooden-built vessel powered by steam. Until you actually see it in motion, it's hard to appreciate how swift and silent it can be. It is also difficult to escape the conclusion that we've progressed backwards since the steam era! The Gondola is a supremely elegant way to travel and to view the mountains but, be warned, passengers at the back sometimes get speckled with soot.

From the jetty, you can look across the lake to the Dunnerdale Fells. Look down the lake, to your left, and you may spot Peel Island. Arthur Ransome set much of his book *Swallows and Amazons* in the countryside around here and on Windermere. Coniston Old Man was 'Kanchenjunga', Belle Isle and Blake-holme island on Windermere were 'Long Island' and 'Wild Cat Island', and Bowness was 'Rio' (which, on reflection, isn't a bad name for the place). Ransome lived in the Coniston area and is buried in the graveyard at Rusland church.

After Parkamoor you climb away from the shore before dropping to meet the reedy foot of the lake, where the water flows into Allan Tarn ('Octopus Lagoon') and then becomes the River Crake (the 'River Amazon'). The road goes through High Nibthwaite – don't blink or you'll miss it – and eventually to a T-junction. Turn right (*Greenodd*, *Ulverston* and *Newby Bridge*), and after crossing a bridge you come almost immediately to a crossroads, just north of the village of Lowick. Turn right towards *Coniston* and the west side of the lake.

LOWICK TO BROUGHTON-IN-FURNESS

You're now on a typical Cumbrian A road – i.e. quick in parts but narrow and twisty when you least expect it. Heading back towards the central Lakes, it passes through the hamlets of Blawith and Water Yeat and across Blawith Common. Look out for the large parking areas after two and a half miles; there's a good walk to the shore of the lake. Half a mile farther on, there is another car-park and public toilets.

The first view of Coniston Water along this stretch is a frustrating one – there are double yellow lines along the road. Half a mile further on, however, you come to a long lay-by beside the lake. In summer there's invariably a strategically parked ice cream van.

After another mile and a half you arrive at the major T-junction in Torver village, just opposite the Wilson's Arms. Turn left (*Broughton-in-Furness*) and head south along the A593.

This is a very round-about way of reaching Broughton-in-Furness; if you look at a map you'll see that you have effectively gone along two sides of a triangle. After four miles or so the attraction of this route becomes obvious – the marvellous views down over the fields to the Duddon Estuary. As you approach Broughton, Black Combe is ahead of you, with the crags of the Dunnerdale Fells marching off to your right. You may be able to spot the railway viaduct over the sands and the narrow church spire in the distance.

Just over six miles from the Torver junction, the road runs alongside park land on your left. Shortly after, you come to a turning on the right for *Ulpha*, *Millom* and *Whitehaven*. If you want to avoid Broughton, turn right here, along a minor road and then right again at the T-junction to rejoin the tour at the High Cross Inn.

Assuming you haven't decided to spurn Broughton, continue along the main road for half a mile, which brings you into Broughton Square.

At the centre of the impressive market square stands a tall obelisk, built in 1810 to commemorate the fiftieth year of the reign of George III. It is flanked by three horse chestnut trees, and on the far side are a pair of butcher's slabs and a set of double stocks.

Entering from the top of the square, the Square Café is on your left and around to your right is Beswick's Restaurant. You can park in the square itself if you want to explore. Exit from the bottom right, by the Manor Arms pub. This takes you down through the town, past a petrol station and Broughton Mountain Centre. Turn right (*Millom* and *Workington*) and go up the side street, past the Black Cock pub, to a T-junction. Turn left, past the church, and you come to another T-junction by the High Cross Inn. The people in the car in front probably took the short cut.

BROUGHTON TO ULPHA

Turn right (*Workington* and *Millom*), on to the A595. As the road drops away there's a tree-covered hillside ahead and, beyond that, Black Combe. Along the valley bottom there is a wonderful view of Coniston Old Man. At the Duddon Bridge traffic lights, turn right (*Ulpha* and *Seathwaite*) into Dunnerdale.

The discovery of iron and copper

Below: The Gondola steam launch, the most elegant way to travel in the Lake District. . . . Opposite: The Coniston fells, viewed from the east shore of the lake, south of Brantwood.

throughout Furness changed the landscape of this area, to the extent that much of it is largely man-made. Eight blast furnaces were set up in the area between 1711 and 1748. The one built by the Duddon Estuary – on the far side of the Duddon Bridge – was established in 1736. It was used to smelt iron ore from the Lindale and Dalton areas. The main fuel was charcoal, which came from the heavily wooded fells. Much of these woods were coppiced, the trees cut short to produce regular saplings to be burnt in pitsteads to form charcoal. At its peak the Duddon furnace needed the charcoal from ten acres of woodland every week, and the cast iron it produced was taken away to Chepstow or Bristol. Duddon furnace stopped making iron in 1867, but a great deal of the original building remains and is now being maintained by the National Park Authority.

Once off the main road there is a steep climb. Below, at the bottom of the wooded valley, is the River Duddon and also a fine Georgian house. This is Duddon Hall. Now the countryside changes and begins to feel wilder, more isolated. The lack of large car-parks, major villages and commercial attractions for visitors has kept the Duddon valley relatively unspoilt, and even on a hot summer day this is a good place to come and escape the crowds. Wordsworth was very fond of this area and wrote a sonnet to the River Duddon.

After a mile and a half, the road crosses a cattle grid and you are out on open fell with a very pretty view into the valley. Hesk Fell is the conical hill directly ahead. When the road descends to the valley bottom there are a few lay-bys – if you fancy a boggy walk down to the river – and a quarry car-park, but there is a better walk farther on.

Three and a half miles into the valley, you cross the Duddon via a small bridge and enter the village of Ulpha.

ULPHA AND DUNNERDALE

The road runs alongside the river for a couple of hundred yards, then bears away from it, past an attractive little dales church. Wordsworth mentioned

The road from Torver to Dunnerdale provides some marvellous views – like this shot from Kiln Bank – but misses out on the chance to visit Broughton and Ulpha.

this in one of his sonnets: 'The Kirk of Ulpha, to the pilgrim's eye, is welcome as a star'. Continue through the village and past the turning for *Eskdale* and *Whitehaven*. This is a very attractive route over Birker Fell to Devoke Water and Eskdale Green, but is rather an extreme detour.

Continuing along the road, the views are disappointingly restricted in places, as you are hemmed in by high walls and hedges. You get the odd glimpse of Stickle Pike on your right and the fell road from Torver. The funny little conical fell just north of the fell road is Caw.

A mile or so from Ulpha, the road bends to the right and crosses the Duddon again. Once over the bridge, the road bears left (*Seathwaite* and *Wrynose*), past a telephone box and turning for Broughton Mills. The view opens out a little, and directly in front is the 'back' view of Coniston Old Man. The eroded path on to Brown Pike is the Walna Scar road, a pack-horse route from Coniston to Seathwaite.

The road passes through Hall Dunnerdale and then starts to meander about in such an extravagant fashion that if it was a river it would have ox-bow bends. Look for the great slabs of bare rock on either side of the road, marked with long scratches or striations, evidence of the passing of glaciers in the last ice age.

Seathwaite in Dunnerdale is not to be confused with the other Seathwaite, in Borrowdale. Apart from anything else, the climate is different – the Borrowdale one boasts that it is the wettest inhabited place in England – average rainfall 130 inches a year. (Before you complain about the weather in the Lake District, just remember that South Devon has a higher annual rainfall than Carlisle.)

Once through Seathwaite, the road climbs again. The Duddon is somewhere below, down amongst the trees. Two and a half miles from Seathwaite – about half a mile after crossing a small humpbacked bridge – there is an open, grassy plateau

on your right. Park here and follow the wooden bridle-way sign opposite and there is a very pleasant, ten-minute walk to the river. The stepping stones, tucked under the canopy of trees, are well worth exploring on a hot summer's day.

Once past the grassy plateau, the distinct hill above the conifer woods on your left is Harter Fell; in front, you can look up the valley towards Bow Fell, with Troutal Fell on your right. Passing places along this stretch tend to get cluttered with parked cars in summer. For some tourists the sight of the river, just across the field, proves too alluring, despite the presence of a barbed wire fence. But if you have already explored the stepping stones you will be able to resist this temptation and drive past, feeling virtuous.

The road drops level with the river and just beyond Troutal Farm there is a stone bridge on your left, just opposite a small larch wood. Carry on to the Forestry Commission car-park and come back on foot for a closer look at the bridge.

This is Birks Bridge, a pack-horse bridge in a picturesque setting on the route which winds over the southern flanks of Harter Fell into Eskdale. It stands over a deep, shady gorge and in summer the pool is an ideal spot for swimming. Diving in is not a good idea, however, as there are a number of submerged rocks.

Possibly to heighten the attractiveness of Birks Bridge and its surroundings, half a mile down the road the Forestry Commission has indulged in an exercise in contrasts by building a set of indescribably ugly concrete houses. Those of a sensitive nature should try not to look as they drive past.

The valley widens into a broad plain and the road meanders through meadows with plenty of visibility ahead to enable you to avoid oncoming traffic. Ahead and to the left you can see Ulpha Fell; to the right, Cockley Beck Fell.

Shortly after passing Black Hall Youth Hostel, you come to a farmhouse and a road junction, where Hardknott Pass comes in from your left. Turn right (*Langdale* and *Wrynose Pass*) and you start to drive along Wrynose Bottom. Passengers might like to entertain the driver with some amusing jokes at this point.

OVER WRYNOSE PASS

A mile and a half along the valley, the road starts to climb. Now the River Duddon, which has been on your left all this time, finally dwindles to a trickle as you climb Wrynose Pass.

Take it steady and remember that you should have right of way if you encounter oncoming traffic (though sometimes going up you get stuck behind someone

Hall Dunnerdale, a tiny settlement mid-way along the valley. There's not even a television aerial to spoil a scene which has changed little over the last 100 years.

who's determined to give way to everyone coming down). At the top you pass the Three Shires Stone, marking the point where the old county boundaries of Lancashire, Westmorland and Cumberland meet. You've just come up from Lancashire and are about to enter Westmorland.

As you start the descent, there is a brilliant view into Little Langdale. Wetherlam is over to your right, Wet Side Edge between the road and Wetherlam. On your left is the southern flank of Pike o'Blisco. Below is the River Brathay, winding down the valley towards Lake Windermere. From this height (around 1,250ft) you can see the Howgills in the distance. Approaching the valley bottom, you get a good view of the Langdale Pikes to your left: Pike o'Stickle, then – working right – Harrison Stickle and Pavey Ark.

LITTLE LANGDALE TO AMBLESIDE

Further down, when the road from Great Langdale comes in from your left, you turn right. Once you've gone over the cattle grid you are officially in Little Langdale. The road gets very narrow at Fell Foot Farm. The innocuous-looking hillock in the field behind the farm is a Viking Thing Mound, or meeting-place. Unfortunately, oblivious of its history, someone seems to have ploughed half of it up.

Once past the farm, you will need to look out for oncoming traffic and passing places – you may need to reverse back to them. This stretch is notoriously tricky and you frequently find yourself in a short queue of cars trying to shuffle past a Mountain Goat minibus.

After two miles, you'll come to a T-junction, signed *Elterwater* left, *Ambleside* and *Coniston* right. Turn right and over a bridge. After a quarter of a mile you come to another T-junction. Turn left (*Ambleside*) and follow the A593 back to Ambleside.

If you're in the Coniston area, don't miss a trip on the Gondola steam launch, possibly the only silent method of powered transport in the Lake District. It was originally launched as a passenger boat in 1859 and ran for 80 years before falling into disuse. It was used as a houseboat for a while but gradually became derelict. Then, in the 1970s, the National Trust recovered it and after lengthy restoration it was relaunched in 1980. The boat carries up to 80 passengers and has luxurious fittings which recapture the splendour of its Victorian heyday. I would certainly recommend a trip though it's worth noting that it can't run in high winds or when the lake is too choppy, so if the weather is poor, ring Coniston tourist information centre to check if the Gondola is sailing.

Coniston Water was the scene of Donald Campbell's fatal attempt on the world water-speed record. Breaking speed records was something of a family tradition; his father, Sir Malcolm Campbell, achieved nine world-speed records on land and three on water and, in 1936, was the first man to travel on land at 300 mph. The name *Bluebird* was another tradition. It was the name of Sir Malcolm's 1936 record-breaking car and Donald Campbell's *Bluebird* was the third boat to bear the name. A three-point hydroplane, it was powered by a Bristol Siddeley Orpheus turbo jet engine, capable of developing 5,000lbs of thrust.

Campbell had already broken the world water-speed record seven times, increasing it to 280 mph on Coniston Water in late 1966. His tragic final attempt took place on 4 January 1967. No one knows quite what happened, but on the final run he achieved over 300 mph before *Bluebird* somersaulted and disintegrated. His body was never found. There is a memorial to him in Coniston village and there are more details about his life and record attempts in the Ruskin Museum in Yewdale Street.

The Old Man of Coniston range.

TOUR SIX
~
Cartmel and the Winster Valley

When staying in the south of Lakeland there is always a tremendous temptation to head north, into the central fells. This tour encourages a little exploration of the delightful countryside around the south-west of Lake Windermere and across to the ancient priory at Cartmel. If the weather is good, and your timing is right, it makes an excellent evening tour on account of the superb view of the sun setting over the Langdale Pikes, on the way home.

Bowness to Cartmel, via a trip on the Windermere ferry and a drive through Finsthwaite and Haverthwaite, returning via Grange-over-Sands, Bowland Bridge and Gummer's How.
Distance: 39 miles. Driving time: 2–3 hours

Lake Windermere concealed beneath a veil of mist, viewed from Gummer's How.

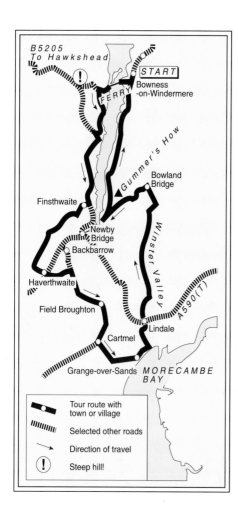

B5205
To Hawkshead

START

Bowness
-on-Windermere

FERRY

Gummer's How

Bowland
Bridge

Finsthwaite

Winster Valley

Newby
Bridge

Backbarrow

A590(T)

Haverthwaite

Field Broughton

Lindale

Cartmel

Grange-over-Sands   MORECAMBE
BAY

Tour route with
town or village

Selected other roads

Direction of travel

Steep hill!

BOWNESS TO FINSTHWAITE

Until the mid-nineteenth century there was no village of Windermere, just Bowness, huddled on the east shore of the lake (and properly called Bowness-on-Windermere, to distinguish it from the other Cumbria Bowness on the Solway coast). Everything changed in 1848 with the arrival of the railway at the tiny hamlet of Birthwaite. The line was originally due to continue to Ambleside, but there was too much local opposition (including angry letters to *The Times* from one William Wordsworth), and so the village of Windermere sprang up where the line stopped. In addition to visitors, the line brought an influx of newcomers. Some of these were wealthy Lancashire businessmen who built grand mansions along the east side of the lake. You'll pass some of them on the return part of the tour.

Head out of Bowness on the A592,

passing the promenade and the boat landings. Glance up at the Belsfield Hotel as you go past; this was once the home of the Furness industrialist, H.W. Schneider. To reach his office he used to commute in his private steam launch to Lakeside and catch a train to Barrow.

After half a mile, turn right (*Hawkshead* and *Coniston via ferry, B5285*) to the car ferry. If there is a queue, don't panic; signs at the roadside tell you how long you have to wait. The ferry capacity is 18 cars, so if you're feeling bored assign a passenger to count the waiting cars. Each crossing (there and back) takes 20 minutes.

Just north of the crossing is Belle Isle, the only inhabited island on Lake Windermere. From the ferry landing you can see the grey dome of a house in the trees. This is the only completely circular house in the country. It was built in 1774, when the island was called Longholme. Seven years later, it was bought by Isabella Curwen, a young Workington heiress, and the island renamed after her. Her husband was John Christian, brother of Fletcher Christian, the famous mutineer on the *Bounty*. John took on the Curwen surname after marriage and Belle Isle remained in the Curwen family until 1991. The island is privately owned, so the only time the public has a better view of the house is in winter, when the leaves have fallen.

As you drive away from the ferry you are on a short peninsula, with moored boats on either side. After a quarter of a mile, the road bears sharp left. (The turning right at this point takes you along the shore to a car-park and if you're staying in Bowness and want to escape the crowds, this makes a good walk. Come across on the ferry as a foot passenger.)

The narrow road climbs steeply away from the lake. At the top of the hill, half a mile from the ferry landing, take the second turning on the left, which brings you on to a narrow minor road. This descends through thick woodland with deer fences along the verge. On a sunny afternoon, the light makes fascinating dappled effects across the road.

High Dam, also known as Finsthwaite Tarn. A delightful spot, with an excellent circular walk around the tarn. A wonderful stroll on a summer's morning.

After a mile and a half, there is a short break in the trees for the houses at High Cunsey. The attractive stream on your left is Cunsey Beck. Shortly after passing Low Cunsey Farm, there is a field on your left and a view of the lake. As there is a slight hill in the way, you occasionally get the bizarre sight of a sail apparently trundling along the top of the field.

This route along the west side of Windermere does not boast the most wonderful views but it is usually quiet and the woods are quite attractive. A mile beyond Low Cunsey Farm, the road climbs steeply and unexpectedly to the top of a gorse and bracken covered fell. There are one or two good public footpaths up here, but the problem is finding somewhere unobtrusive to park.

Follow the road to a T-junction and go left (*Lakeside* and *Newby Bridge*). Opposite the junction are the gates to Graythwaite Hall. During the early summer, the walled grounds are open to the public. The wall ends and you pass Graythwaite Old Hall, with its rather fine topiary hedge. Just opposite is Silver Holme, a guest house which takes its name from one of Windermere's smaller islands. Ransome enthusiasts will know it as 'Cormorant Island'.

After another two miles, there's a turning to the right which goes uphill. Continue past and you will see a sign for Stott Park Bobbin Mill. The road goes uphill, past the Bobbin Mill, and bears left by a large white house. You want to take the sharp turning on the right (*Finsthwaite, Rusland* and *Satterthwaite*) to go round the back of the mill and past the car-park.

From the road the mill looks like nothing more than a red brick chimney and a few corrugated iron sheds, but appearances are deceptive. This is one of the most interesting – and surprising – of the Lake District's historical sites, and it is open to the public.

Continue along the road into

Finsthwaite. As you pass the village sign, look out for a track on your right, signed *Public Footpath High Dam*. This leads to a small car-park from which you can walk uphill to a delightful little reservoir encircled by low, wooded hills. It is a miniature Tarn Hows without the crowds.

You will encounter a number of villages ending in '-thwaite' in the Lakes; it is an old Norse word meaning a clearing in the forest. Finsthwaite is a pretty little village, though I have my doubts about St Peter's church. It looks as though the architects had a squabble half way through its construction and the tower ends with a sort of spire. It's in a lovely location, surrounded by fields, but I can't help thinking that it looks like a bit left over from *Thunderbirds*.

Three-quarters of a mile beyond the village you come to a crossroads and the possibility of a detour.

DETOUR TO NEWBY BRIDGE
If you want to explore Newby Bridge and have a look at the River Leven, go left. At Newby Bridge turn right on to the A590 and, just beyond the dual carriageway, left up through Backbarrow to rejoin the tour at Bigland Hall. This is quite pretty – and you get a view of the steam railway line – but the road junction at Newby Bridge is extremely awkward as the A590 is a very fast stretch of road.

FINSTHWAITE TO HAVERTHWAITE
If you are not taking the detour, go right at the crossroads (*Satterthwaite* and *Rusland*) and climb through the woods before descending to a view into the southern end of Rusland Valley. At the T-junction, turn left (*Haverthwaite* and *Ulverston*) and you are out in more open countryside with a wooded fell on your left. This is a good, wide minor road with a pleasant view across the valley. Just past

the Cobblestones Restaurant take the turning on the left (*Haverthwaite* and *Ulverston*), meandering down to the A590.

If you want to look at steam trains, go left along the A590 for about half a mile and you'll come to the main Lakeside-Haverthwaite railway depot. The railway is run by local enthusiasts using the only remaining part of the line which used to link Lakeside to Ulverston.

The tour goes straight across (*B5278, Cark*) and takes you through the village of Haverthwaite. It can be tricky crossing the A590, so take care. The road passes under an old railway bridge and, less than a mile from the main road, crosses a bridge over the River Leven. Immediately over the bridge, turn left (*Low Wood* and *Bigland Hall*), past a small art gallery and workshop, and zigzag up a very narrow, wooded lane. Once out of the trees, the second turning on the left is the road leading up from Backbarrow, and this is where the detour to Newby Bridge rejoins the route.

HAVERTHWAITE TO CARTMEL PRIORY
Bigland Hall, on your right, is a very old estate which now offers various country sports, such as riding, archery and fishing (they even have their own tarn).

A mile and a half past the estate you pass a new-looking barn and turn left, following the sign to *Lindale* and *Grange*.

As you descend into Cartmel Valley, the low, grey-green ridge ahead of you is Hampsfell (or Hampsfield Fell according to the Ordnance Survey), a long limestone escarpment running down to the sea at Grange-over-Sands. Although the summit is only 272ft high, it has the most spectacular all-round view; south to Blackpool, west to the Isle of Man, north to Skiddaw and east to Ingleborough in the Yorkshire Dales.

Ignoring turnings for Wood Broughton, after a mile you come to a T-junction.

Right: Sheep in the Winster Valley, wondering if photographers are edible. Below: The stone sign at Cartmel, formerly the quickest route to Lancaster was across Morecambe Bay.

On the left is the tall spire of the church at Field Broughton. Turn right (there's no sign) and follow the road along the bottom of the valley to Cartmel.

After another mile look out for a white painted milestone, in the grass verge, bearing the words *Hawkshead 13 miles*. It is at the junction with the road from High Newton.

Once past the turning for Aynsome Manor, the road runs beside an attractive park on your left and you come to Cartmel. Take the second turning on the right, just next to the Spar shop and the Pig and Whistle pub.

At the next T-junction, go right again. As you make the turning, look out for the white sign in the wall, opposite the bus stop. This gives distances to Lancaster and Ulverston and dates from the days when the main route into the area was across the Kent Estuary and the sands of Morecambe Bay.

The road takes you past the entrance to Cartmel Priory, and over a narrow bridge into Cartmel Square. Avoid parking in the square, it ruins the view. Use the car-park on the racecourse, just down the narrow lane to the left of the post office.

Cartmel is a lovely village, a bit like Hawkshead but not as twee. Until the nineteenth century, it was known as Cartmel Churchtown. The Priory was founded by William Marshall, Earl of Pembroke, in 1189, and the Gatehouse was built around 1340 (probably to defend the Priory against raiders from Scotland). Only the Gatehouse and part of the chapel remain from the original buildings. A troop of Cromwell's soldiers camped in the Priory one night in 1643 and peppered the nail-studded door at the south-west aisle with bullets. You can still see the holes.

The focal point of the square is the old market cross, together with the water pump and trough. It's a pity about the mock Regency litter bin, right next to

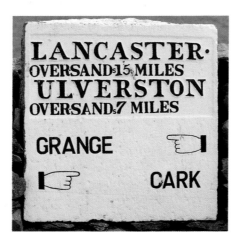

them. Saunter left, under Cartmel Gatehouse, and follow the narrow back lane which leads around the village, circling back to the main street via the Priory grounds. Look out for the old green metal sign advertising 'Raleigh the All Steel Bicycle'. (There is a similar one in Ravenglass on the fourth tour.)

Cartmel is the home of the famous Cartmel Races, which are held on spring and late summer bank holidays.

After stretching your legs, and perhaps visiting one of the cafés, you should be ready for the next part of the tour. In case you were wondering, you are about half-way round.

CARTMEL TO GRANGE-OVER-SANDS

Drive back to the main road at the Pig and Whistle and turn right, then immediately left and left again, following signs for *Grange-over-Sands*. If you have sharp

eyes you may notice an interesting old water pump in the wall opposite the pub.

There is a footpath sign for Hampsfell at the top of the hill, half a mile from the village.

After a mile, turn left (*Grange-over-Sands town centre* and *Golf Club*). A short climb is followed by a steep drop into Grange-over-Sands. This descent has a terrific view across Morecambe Bay. The wooded knoll across the other side of the estuary is Arnside Knott. Work round to the right and you can see the Morecambe and Heysham atomic power station. Follow the coastline and on a clear day you may spot Blackpool Tower. In autumn this is also a very pretty view at night, during the Blackpool and Morecambe illuminations.

At the T-junction by the library turn left and follow the road to another T-junction, beside the church. Turn left, past the clocktower and then left again, down through the parade of shops. The road goes past the Ornamental Gardens and another row of covered shops with attractive wrought ironwork. It then bears right, past Bateman's Garage, to the railway station.

If you are in need of more fresh air, this is a good point to stop and explore. If you go right, in front of the station, you reach the Ornamental Gardens. Alternatively, go under the bridge to the left of the station (preferably without your car) and you are on Grange Promenade. Across the estuary you can see the Kent Viaduct, where the railway line crosses the sands at Arnside.

Grange was little more than a tiny hamlet until the arrival of the railway in 1857. Then, thanks to its moderate temperature and fresh sea air, it rapidly became a fashionable Victorian holiday resort.

GRANGE TO BOWLAND BRIDGE

Back in the car, the road takes you around the foot of Hampsfell and past another golf club. Across the fields to your right is a tiny wooded knoll called Castle Head, believed to have once been the site of a Roman fort.

As you enter Lindale, look out for the

black iron obelisk on your right, a memorial to John 'Iron Mad' Wilkinson. He lived in the large house at Castle Head.

At the crossroads, just opposite the Lindale Inn, go straight across. No, not into the pub but down the narrow lane on its right. Turn right at the next junction, under the bypass, meandering along the pretty lane which follows the contours of Cartmel Fell. To your right, across the Winster Valley, is the wooded limestone escarpment of Whitbarrow Scar. Look carefully and you might spot the tower at Witherslack Hall, lurking among the trees.

At the next crossroads, a mile from Lindale, go straight across (*Cartmel Fell*). The small reedy pond in the fields is Helton Tarn. There are plenty of farms, so be wary of mud on the road after rain and watch out for sheepdogs; they don't take kindly to having to move

out of the way of passing traffic. You will pass loads of public footpath signs, but if you decide to park, do choose somewhere where you won't cause traffic problems and make sure you have an Ordnance Survey map, or you may never find your car again.

You will pass a turning for High Newton and a mile or so later arrive at the T-junction at Hodge Hill. Go right (*Kendal*), and you are now travelling away from Cartmel Fell, past fields. Half a mile later you reach another T-junction where you go left (*Bowland Bridge* and *Kendal*). Cartmel Fell is now in front of you. Watch out for the wonderfully named Burblethwaite Mill, shortly before you arrive at Bowland Bridge and another T-junction, between a pair of white houses.

GUMMER'S HOW

If you went right here you could pass the Hare and Hounds pub, opposite the

village store and petrol pump (not a petrol station, note). This road eventually joins the A5074 at Winster and is a quick way back to Bowness.

However, the tour goes left, and across the bridge. Select low gear. This steep hill in front of you is known as Strawberry Bank and was once a pack-horse route. As you climb past the Mason's Arms pub the road suddenly gets very steep and there's a hairpin bend, just to make things interesting. It rivals anything you might encounter on Hardknott Pass. Keep well into your side of the road – the two pubs are very popular and there is likely to be plenty of traffic even out of season.

Excitement over, you can look back down the valley to Whitbarrow Scar and the estuary. After another two miles, you come to a one-in-six descent and a tremendous view of the southern basin of Lake Windermere.

There is a Forestry Commission carpark, half a mile downhill. If you are feeling energetic, you can walk across the road and up to a kissing gate. After a stiff, fifteen minute walk you arrive at the top of Gummer's How. It is only 1,054ft high, but from the triangulation point at the summit you get wonderful panoramas south to Ulverston and north to the central Lakeland fells.

Alternatively, if it is blowing a gale, and you've left the cagoules in the boot, continue downhill for another hundred yards and there is a lay-by which gives a maximum of four lazy drivers an excellent view of the lake. On the far shore is Lakeside and the steamer pier. Search inland and you may spot the red brick chimney of Stott Park Bobbin Mill in the woods.

From this view point, look south and along the River Leven to Newby Bridge. If you see steam rising from the trees, the Haverthwaite railway must be running. Beyond that, in the distance, you may spot a tall tower, standing on a hill above Ulverston. This is the Hoad Monument, built in memory of Sir John Barrow, the Arctic explorer and a founder of the Royal Geographical Society. It was built in 1850 and is a 100ft high replica of the Eddystone lighthouse.

Setting off again, the road descends steeply to the junction with the A592. There is another hand-painted sign in the wall on your right. Turn right (*Bowness*) on to the final leg of the tour.

GUMMER'S HOW TO BOWNESS

Fellfoot Park – on the left – was once the grounds of a private house but is now owned by the National Trust. It is a pleasant place to wander through on your way down to the lake on a summer evening, but can get busy during the day.

The next stretch of road (as you come alongside the field and a view of Lakeside) looks narrower than it is, but you might feel like grinding to a halt if confronted by a coach.

The A592 to Bowness is very pretty in autumn, just as the leaves begin to turn. It is also an attractive route on a summer evening. After three miles you will see why: you round a right-hand bend and then, without warning, come upon a lay-by and a superb view of the Langdales. Catch this at sunset and it can be spectacular. If the lay-by is full, carry on to the National Park car-park, just prior to the Beech Hill Hotel.

Once past the Beech Hill the trees block the view. After a mile and a half, you pass the Storr's Hall Hotel. This was once a private home, and slaves were landed at Barrow and brought here before continuing down into North Lancashire. Rumour has it that there are still chains in the basement. Ironically, just across the lake was the home of William Wilberforce, the anti-slave trade campaigner. If you use a bar lunch as an excuse, you can wander through the grounds down to a strange stone building, projecting into the lake. This is known as the Temple of Heroes and was a meeting-place for Wordsworth and his chums.

Continue along the A592, which takes you past the turning for the ferry and back into Bowness.

This is an excellent tour for an afternoon, perhaps combining it with an evening pub meal. Areas like the Lakes and Dales are well served with pubs, some of which offer remarkably good meals. The Mason's Arms on Cartmel Fell imports exotic beers from around the world and even runs its own brewery.

On a good day, viewed from Gummer's How, the sunset over the Langdales can be truly spectacular. You don't even have to climb the mountain – there's a good lay-by just below the main car-park which provides a good view. This is a good vantage point to watch the 'steamers' at Lakeside. Few visitors realize that Lake Windermere is actually a public highway with its own navigation rules, regulations and speed limits. Today it is used primarily for pleasure, but the car-ferry, which runs across the width of the lake at its narrowest point, runs all year round for the benefit of commuters, starting at around 6.30 am and running a regular service until around 10.00 pm.

There are a couple of other boat services on Windermere, the oldest of which is the Windermere Iron Steamboat Company, first established in 1848. It runs the large, rather grand-looking cruisers which you may see navigating the lake, from Waterhead in the north to Lakeside in the south. It's worth a detour to Lakeside to see the boats, especially when they come in to dock. There is also a small steam railway line, linking Lakeside to Haverthwaite, which was once part of a branch line to Ulverston.

As you continue the tour, you eventually reach Cartmel, a charming village which has not been as overwhelmed with tourism as Hawkshead, and which continues to be a living village, rather than becoming a museum piece. The priory is a magnificent building and it's worth making a special trip to the village if you are around on a bank holiday Saturday or Monday. This is when the Cartmel races are held on the smallest National Hunt course in Britain.

The Mason's Arms, Cartmel Fell.

TOUR SEVEN
~
Cockermouth and the Solway Coast

The coast of Cumbria is unjustly

neglected by most visitors to the Lake

District. While it lacks the obvious scale

and drama of the Lakeland fells and lakes,

it has isolated beaches, a rich variety of

wildlife and traces of some of the most

turbulent events in English history.

This tour explores some of the towns and

coastal villages along the Solway Firth and

gives you the opportunity to visit Carlisle,

the region's ancient capital and now the

county town of Cumbria.

Exploring the coast from Cockermouth and Maryport,
through Allonby, Silloth and Holm Cultram Abbey – then
around to Bowness-on-Solway and Burgh by Sands, and
back via Carlisle, Bassenthwaite Lake and Isel.
Distance: 89 miles. Driving time: 3½ hours

The beach at Allonby, a famous Victorian resort.
It is now designated an Area of Outstanding Natural Beauty.

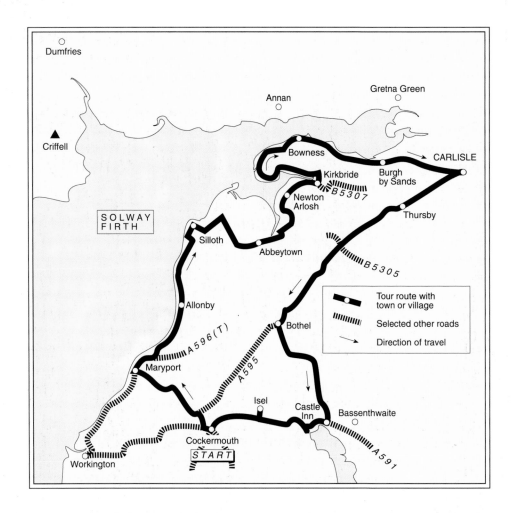

COCKERMOUTH

This lively market town lies just outside the Lake District, excluded by an unkind wiggle in the National Park's boundary. Nevertheless it's an unspoilt, attractive place and one of Cumbria's most historic towns. There was a settlement here in the Iron Age, and the Romans built a fort at the nearby junction of the Roman roads to Maryport, Penrith and Carlisle. Cockermouth Castle was built in 1250 (it is now privately owned by Lord Egremont) and the town's basic street plan has remained unchanged since medieval times.

It is easy to spend an hour or two poking about in the antique shops or wandering up the side streets, looking at some of the fine, Georgian town houses. William and Dorothy Wordsworth were born in Cockermouth, and the family home – now known as Wordsworth House – is owned by the National Trust and open to the public. Another notable resident was Fletcher Christian, the famous mutineer of the *Bounty*.

COCKERMOUTH TO MARYPORT

Travel west along the main street, past Wordsworth House and the Kingfisher Inn, to the mini-roundabout. Take the second exit (*Maryport* and *Carlisle*) to go across the River Cocker and head out of town. A mile later there is a grown-up roundabout; go straight across (*Maryport*) on to the A594. About five miles from Cockermouth, the drive begins to get interesting: as you start to approach Maryport, the sea comes into view and you can see Criffel, on the far side of the Solway Firth.

Maryport has tried hard to put itself on the tourist map in recent years. This is not very apparent when you drive through the outskirts, but it's worth persevering. At the crossroads and traffic lights go left (*Workington*), along Curzon Street, and the second turning on the right (*Town Centre, Maritime Steamships, Harbour*

One of the horses from Allonby Riding School, allowed to roam free along the shore. In the background, across the Solway Firth, is the distinctive shape of Criffel.

and *Tourist Information*) takes you up Senhouse Street and down to the harbour.

Drive over the bridge and you can park by the harbour wall. This area has been extensively redeveloped in recent years, but there has been a harbour here ever since the Romans built a fort, Alauna, on the clifftops. Since 1570 the Senhouse family has been preserving some of the best Roman finds, and these are displayed in a museum near the site of the fort.

In 1749, Humphrey Senhouse built a quay to ship coal from his estates. He developed the nearby village of Ellenfoot and renamed it after his wife, Mary. In 1867 over 3,000 ships used the port. The last locally registered ship was launched here in 1952. There is a fascinating little Maritime Museum in the tourist information centre, on the right as you go back over the bridge.

To find the Roman museum, which is very badly signposted, go back up the hill and turn left into High Street (*All Through Traffic* and *Senhouse Roman Museum*). Carry on to the top and go right, through Fleming Square, and then left, along Christian Street. Keep going until you reach the Promenade, then go right, to the museum.

If after all that the museum is closed, don't throw the book over the cliff – go and admire the view. The museum stands on the cliff edge, overlooking Maryport and the harbour, with a brilliant view of Criffel and the Galloway hills.

Returning along the Promenade, turn left where you came in, follow Christian Street all the way down and turn left into Wood Street to get back to the junction with the traffic lights. Turn left (*Carlisle, Allonby* and *Silloth*).

MARYPORT TO SILLOTH
Three-quarters of a mile along, turn left (*Silloth*). Criffel and the Galloway hills

stay with you for the next seven miles as the B5300 runs alongside the beach. There are numerous parking places but the most interesting place to stop is just after the turning for Crosscanonby, in a long lay-by beside the embankment. Pull in here for a quick history lesson.

The Crosscanonby Salt Pans must be one of the earliest industrial sites in Cumbria. They were established by the Normans to extract salt from sea water, a complicated process explained by an excellent little information panel in the lay-by. The site fell into disuse around 1730.

Go up the steps and you come to the site of a Roman fortlet, part of the coastal defences which protected Cumbria's western flanks from marauding Celts who used coracles to try to sneak round Hadrian's Wall by sea. The site has only recently been excavated and there is a wooden viewing platform, to give you

some idea of the layout.

Two miles beyond the Salt Pans is the village of Allonby, a fashionable bathing resort in the late eighteenth century, although you might find this hard to believe. Here Charles Dickens and Wilkie Collins stayed at the Ship Inn whilst on a walking holiday in 1857. Look out for horses wandering across the road. They belong to Allonby Riding School and are allowed to roam free over the village green. It makes a change from the usual Lakeland driving hazard of slowing down for sheep.

The coast along here is subject to constant erosion, so there have been a number of measures to try and conserve it. These include building board walks, erecting sand fences and seeding murran grass along the cliffs. If you build any sand-castles, make sure you empty out your bucket when you leave because it is actually illegal to remove any sand.

The monument to Edward I overlooking the Solway Firth at Burgh by Sands. The pillar was restored and enclosed by Sir George Henry, 4th Earl of Lonsdale, in 1876.

SILLOTH TO ABBEYTOWN

The route into Silloth is along a very wide cobbled street which leads to a cross-roads. To the left is Carr's Flour Mill (a family business which originated in Carlisle in 1831) and straight ahead is a car-park. Turn right, down Criffel Street and pull in by the Park.

The Victorians intended Silloth to become a major port, and a rail link to Carlisle was opened in 1856, but it was as a tourist resort that the town really took off. In 1900 it was *the* fashionable place to be seen in Cumbria, and until 1939 it even had a steamer service to Dublin and the Isle of Man.

The Park features a small amusement arcade and a little train, which trundles across the grass at weekends. There is also a long esplanade, and although the place has a certain, faded charm the overall effect is slightly bizarre, like something out of a Ray Bradbury novel. The tourist information centre is in a wooden hut by the road.

Carry on along Criffel Street and look out for a turning to the right (*Abbeytown*, *Wigton* and *Carlisle*) – it is easy to miss this as the sign may be obscured by branches. As you leave town, the sight of the large electronics factory on your left is offset by the view of the Lakeland hills in the distance to your right.

After two and a half miles you pass through the hamlet of Calvo and have an even better view of Skiddaw and Blencathra, with no factories to distract you. Shortly afterwards, you come to Abbeytown.

HOLM CULTRAM ABBEY

When the road bears right, a short distance along the street, you want to go straight on for *Newton Arlosh* and *Kirkbride* (the sign is not easy to spot), past the Wheatsheaf Inn to the ruins of Holm Cultram Abbey.

The Abbey was founded in 1150 and suffered in the Border raids. Robert the

Bruce sacked it in 1319, despite the fact that his father was buried here. In between raids, the monks were a busy lot, establishing a port at Skinburness, running the salt works, reclaiming land. At the time of the Dissolution of the Monasteries, in 1536–9, the locals successfully petitioned Cromwell for what remained of the Abbey to be preserved as a church and a refuge from raiders. It has gradually sunk into neglect, but the parish church still remains, in the old nave of the Abbey.

ABBEYTOWN TO BOWNESS-ON-SOLWAY

The road bears left, past the Abbey and a farm. Then you see what appears to be a plantation of radio masts. This is a transmitter station operated by the Royal Navy.

After three miles you come into Newton Arlosh. To the left is the church, which bears witness to the region's turbulent history; it incorporates a pele tower. The village was created by the monks at Holm Cultram after their settlement at Skinburness had been washed away by storms in 1305.

Go straight through the village and within another two miles you come to Kirkbride. You can see the mouth of the River Whampool on your left as you go over a small bridge. Take the turning on the left for *Whitrigg* and *Bowness-on-Solway*, which takes you over the river to a T-junction.

Turn left (*Longcroft* and *Anthorn*) on to the narrow coastal road which goes past the transmitter masts. The sheep grazing in the fields at the foot of the masts make an extremely odd contrast. Look over your left shoulder and you can see back to Grune Point at Skinburness and, a little farther round, Skiddaw and the Lakeland fells. As you drive past the

masts, the mud flats of Moricambe Bay are on your left. This is an area rich in bird life, including oyster-catchers, plovers and dunlins. As you continue through Cardurnock – three houses and a cat – you can see Annan and the power station on the far side of the Solway.

Four miles after Cardurnock, as you approach Bowness-on-Solway, look out for an embankment jutting out into the estuary. This is the remains of a railway viaduct, an ambitious venture which was designed to link the iron ore mines of West Cumbria with the steel works at Lanark, in Scotland. It opened in 1869 as a branch line which left the Maryport–Carlisle Railway at Kirkbride to join the Caledonian line just east of Ecclefechan. The viaduct was over a mile long and stood on 193 cast-iron pillars which were protected from the shifting sands by wooden buttresses.

It was a very optimistic enterprise; the sands of the Solway proved far too unstable to support it, and in the exceptionally hard winter of 1881, 45 of the pillars were carried away by ice floes. It closed in 1921, by which time the iron ore mines were running down and there was no financial incentive to keep it repaired. The viaduct was demolished 14 years later.

BOWNESS-ON-SOLWAY TO BURGH BY SANDS

For the next few miles – until you reach Burgh by Sands – the road runs parallel with the line of Hadrian's Wall. Designed to keep out the hostile Scots, the Wall was built in AD 122, originally as a turf embankment, which stretched from Wallsend, on the Tyne, through Carlisle to a Roman fort at Bowness-on-Solway. It was rebuilt in stone a few years later, but the Romans never did get round to modernizing the stretch west of Carlisle.

The next village was originally called Fisher's Cross but became Port Carlisle in 1823 when a canal linked it to Carlisle. You can see the remains of the harbour embankment across the marshy field to the left, as you enter the village.

Two miles from Port Carlisle you come into the hamlet of Drumburgh. Don't be put off by the unremarkable bungalows – as you leave the village there's a lovely old building on your right, Drumburgh Castle Farm. The castle is a pele tower, built in 1307 (using stone filched from Hadrian's Wall) to guard one of the major fords across the Solway. It was rebuilt and extended as a farmhouse in the sixteenth century.

After three miles of very straight road, you pass through Dykesfield and come to Burgh by Sands. Go past the Greyhound Inn to the crossroads and turn left, on to a minor road (*Sandsfield*).

After half a mile, look out for a narrow track on the left, signed *Public Footpath to King Edward I Monument* and *Old Sandside*. There would be a car-park here if someone hadn't dumped a load of earth all over it. However, you can just squeeze the car in next to the right-hand track without obstructing the farm gate, and if you look across the fields you will see a strange, tall pillar in the distance. Dig out your wellies and get ready for a walk.

The path goes down the right-hand track and crosses a muddy field to a stile (it's in the hedge, slightly to the right). This takes you to a 25 ft high monument, surrounded by iron railings, which stands alone in the centre of a field on the edge of Burgh Marsh.

In 1300, King Edward I took an army of 6,000 men over the Solway in retaliation for three separate invasions by the Scots. He campaigned in Galloway, capturing Caerlaverock Castle, using Skinburness as his naval supply base. He returned in 1306 to sort out Robert the Bruce and conducted his Parliament from Carlisle. His third venture was less successful; old and ill, he was carried by horse litter from Carlisle and died in this field on 7 July 1307. His body was buried at Westminster but, the art of the mortician being what it was in the fourteenth century, his entrails were buried at Holm Cultram Abbey.

There is a tremendous sense of history here, and standing in the windswept field today, looking out over the Solway, it is not hard to imagine the horses, tents and confusion of a major campaign in progress.

BURGH BY SANDS TO CARLISLE

Driving back to Burgh by Sands you may be astonished to spot a thatched cottage, an extremely rare sight in Cumbria. Back at the junction, turn left, along the main street (*Kirkandrews* and *Carlisle*) and past the twelfth-century church with its fourteenth-century pele tower.

The road goes through Monkhill to Kirkandrews on Eden, a pleasant collection of farms, interspersed with chestnut trees and especially pretty in autumn. Just north of the village, the River Eden makes a broad loop on its way to the Solway, having travelled from Black Fell Moss on the Pennines.

A mile out of Kirkandrews, the road goes over the line of an old railway and you can see Carlisle ahead. After another mile, you come to a T-junction. Turn left (*Carlisle*) and the B5307 brings you to the roundabout on the A595.

Now you have a choice: Carlisle is left (*City Centre*) but if you want to get back to Cockermouth, go round to the third exit and follow the signs for *A595* and *Workington*.

CARLISLE

If the lure of Cumbria's capital proves too great, go left at the roundabout and the broad dual carriageway takes you past Carlisle Castle.

Our advice for navigating around the city is quite simple: don't. There are two pay-and-display car-parks either side of the castle and we recommend that you make use of one of them (the second is short stay). Then use the subway to walk under the dual carriageway and follow any of the streets into the centre.

Carlisle is the administrative centre of Cumbria, but most day visitors come here for the shops or to visit the castle and the museums. It is a very ancient city. The Romans built a town here to serve as the garrison for Stanwix, the nearby fort on Hadrian's Wall. The town was still a Saxon stronghold at the time of the Norman conquest and is said to be the only town in England to preserve its original, British name – Caer-Luel.

After the Normans captured the town, in 1092, they built a castle and for the next seven hundred years it was the focal point in the struggle for territory between Scotland and England. It now houses the Border Regiment Museum and is open to the public, but the best place to find out about the Border wars and the history of the area is the very impressive new Tullie House Museum.

Also well worth visiting is the cathedral which, although small, is perfectly formed and stands in one of the oldest and most attractive parts of the city.

CARLISLE TO COCKERMOUTH

Once you've had your fill of bright lights, rejoin the dual carriageway and head back to the roundabout. The *Workington* exit takes you out of the city along the course of a Roman road and after four miles you come to another roundabout; take the second exit (*Keswick* and *Cockermouth*) to stay on the A595.

You can follow the A595 all the way back to Cockermouth; but for a more interesting route, turn left just past the turning for Bothel (seven miles south of Wigton) on to the A591 (*Keswick*). After a mile you get a wonderful view of our old friends, the Lakeland fells. Skiddaw is directly in front, with Blencathra and the Caldbeck fells to the left, Grisedale Pike and Grasmoor to the right.

Four and a half miles further on, you come to the crossroads at the Castle Inn Hotel. Go right (*Bassenthwaite* and *Cockermouth*), on to the B5291, and as you approach the Armathwaite Hotel you can see Bassenthwaite Lake.

Once across the Ouse Bridge, over the River Derwent – less than a quarter of a mile past the lay-by – abandon the B5291 by turning right (*Higham Hall* and *Embleton*). After another quarter of a mile, go right again (*Isel*) on to an even narrower road. Two and a half miles along this pleasant back route, you can take a short detour by turning right for *Blindcrake*, *Sunderland* and *Isel*. This takes you to a lovely little church on the opposite bank of the Derwent.

Leaving the church, go back over the bridge to the junction, turn right and the road eventually brings you into Cockermouth.

In the right conditions, at the right time of year, this drive can be wonderful. Do it on a windy, overcast day, or when the drizzle is blowing horizontally across the road and you might want to throw the book out of the car window! This is a peaceful and unspoilt coastline with good roads and enjoyable driving, though the section beyond Newton Arlosh can sometimes be hazardous, flooding during exceptionally high tides. Look out for the depth warnings, just past Bowness-on-Solway.

History was never my strong point at school – I gave it up to do rowing – but as I get older, the more interested I become in the past. The Solway coast has a rich and sometimes violent history going back centuries. It was the subject of many battles and skirmishes between the Scots and the English. Perhaps the most poignant reminder of this is Edward I's monument, standing alone in a field at Burgh by Sands. The Salt Pans at Crosscanonby are really fascinating too – a good piece of restoration work by Cumbria County Council – and you also get a good feel for the history of the region at the excellent Tullie House Museum, in Carlisle.

If you blink it is easy to miss Port Carlisle. Try to find the old harbour wall, dating from the days when a canal linked the village with Carlisle. It was the idea of marine architect, William Chapman, (whose real ambition was to link the Irish and North Seas via a canal which crossed the Tyne Gap). The Carlisle and Annan Navigation Company was formed in 1819 and, four years later, a canal was opened. It was eleven miles long, with a drop of 60ft, navigated by eight locks, and was built at a cost of £90,000. It connected with steamer services to Liverpool and Annan, but there was never enough traffic to keep it profitable and it was killed off by the railways. In 1848 the Navigation Company decided to throw in the towel, changed its name to Railway Company and turned the canal into a railway line!

A salt counter's grave, Crosscanonby.

TOUR EIGHT
~
Alston and Hadrian's Wall

This is a tour of magnificent contrasts:
along the gentle, rolling farmland of the
Eden Valley to the windswept moors of the
Pennines. On the way you encounter
historic villages, elegant ruins, a wild,
isolated stretch of Hadrian's Wall and
England's highest market town. This route
contains some of the most breath-taking
scenery in Cumbria and what is possibly
the best tea-shop in the whole book . . .

Penrith to Brampton, via Edenhall, Kirkoswald and Castle
Carrock, then along Hadrian's Wall to Gilsland and back
via Lambley, Alston and Melmerby.
Distance: 67 miles. Driving time: 4–5 hours

Lanercost Priory, founded by the Augustinians,
has suffered over the centuries in the Border wars.

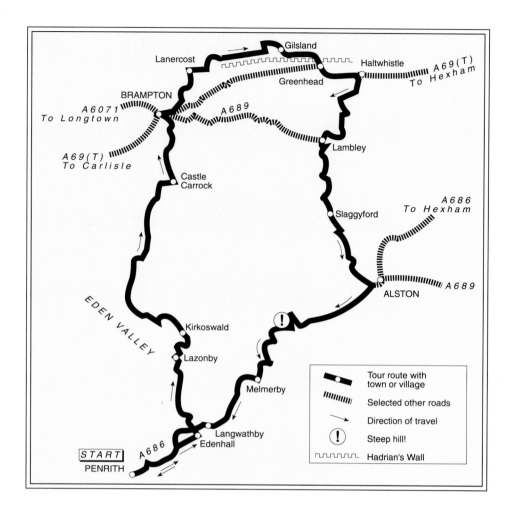

Tour route with town or village
Selected other roads
Direction of travel
Steep hill!
Hadrian's Wall

PENRITH

Penrith is a busy, thriving market town that, despite being less than five miles from Ullswater, feels quite separate from the Lake District. This is partly due to the rust-coloured sandstone that features in so many of the buildings, but also to the fact that Penrith always relied on farming and industry, rather than tourism, for its prosperity.

The town grew up by the major crossing point on the River Eamont. The Romans established a fort nearby, on the road between Carlisle and York. After Edward I seized the region for England in 1295, the town suffered long centuries of skirmishes between the Scots and the English. The castle – now a rather dilapidated ruin – was built in 1397 but was only in use for a couple of centuries; by the sixteenth, most of its brickwork had found its way into the neighbouring houses. A market charter was granted to

Penrith by Henry III in 1223, and the site of the original market cross is commemorated by the clocktower in Market Place.

St Andrew's church lies behind King's Street. In the churchyard is the Giant's Grave, a combination of two eleventh-century crosses and four hogback tombstones. It is reputed to be the grave of Owen Caesarius, the tenth-century King of Cumbria.

Standing on the forested hill to the north of town is Penrith Beacon, a sandstone tower built in the eighteenth century. Beacon Hill is only 937ft high but it was once part of a chain of sites – established in the mid-fifteenth century – where bonfires were lit to warn of raids from across the border.

PENRITH TO EDENHALL

Penrith's one-way system is far too difficult to describe, so we are going to

shirk our responsibilities and suggest you follow the signs for *Kendal* and *A6 South* to the main roundabout on the A6, just south of town. The tour starts here.

Take the first exit (*Alston, A686*) and as you drive along the outskirts of town, look left and you can spot the Beacon. Directly ahead is Cross Fell, at 2,930ft the highest point on the Pennines. The white dot to the right is the British Airports Authority tracking station.

After two and a half miles, turn right for *Edenhall village*. Go down the narrow lane, past Whinsfield Farm and a stretch of mixed woodland, and you suddenly come to a pair of impressive sandstone pillars.

The route goes left (*Edenhall* and *Langwathby*) but it is worth pausing to examine the carved, armoured limbs on top of the columns. These are part of the coat of arms of the Musgrave family, who lived at Edenhall from 1460 to 1900. The gates mark the entrance to their manor house, built in 1821 by Robert Smirke, who also designed the British Museum. It was finally auctioned off and demolished in 1934. The name Edenhall means 'a piece of flat land by the river'.

Follow the signs into Edenhall village, passing Home Farm on the right. Look out for the clocktower through the second entrance. The Musgrave family arms are repeated on the semi-detached cottages opposite. At the war memorial the road bears left, but there is a lane leading to the church on the right and this is worth a diversion. St Cuthbert's stands just above the village, overlooking fields and the River Eden. It is a lovely, secluded spot with view up to Cross Fell, Mickle Fell and the northern Pennines.

EDENHALL TO KIRKOSWALD

Return to the war memorial and continue past the Edenhall Hotel to the crossroads at the A686. Go straight across (*Great Salkeld, Lazonby*) on to another country lane. As you cross you may spot the iron road bridge over the Eden, on your right.

After half a mile turn right at the T-junction to join the B6412, a very pretty road through neat pastures and crop fields, with the occasional flash of the

Eden glimpsed on your right. It feels quite unlike anything in the central Lakes. A mile and a half from the junction, you will go past to Nunwick Hall. Look out for the interesting gateposts.

The villages of Great and Little Salkeld lie west and east of the River Eden. Our route takes us through Great Salkeld, past another St Cuthbert's church and, after a mile of winding road, into Lazonby village.

At the T-junction, in the village centre, turn right (*Kirkoswald* and *Brampton*) and this take you under the Settle–Carlisle railway line (Lazonby station is behind the hotel). As you leave the village, you approach the river again and can see the elegant, sandstone Eden Bridge. There is a car-park if you want to admire the view.

Kirkoswald simply means 'Oswald's church', named after the King of Northumbria (there is more about this enterprising monarch in the eleventh tour). As you approach the village you can see the church across the fields on your right. It is set some distance back from the road, and the only way to get to it is to park in the village and return on foot.

The approach to the church is along Priest's Walk, a flagged path, through an avenue of lime trees. The position of the church, the earliest parts of which date from the twelfth and thirteenth centuries, was determined by the location of a holy well, dedicated to St Oswald. You can still find the well to the right of the church door; there is a cast-iron lid and a metal cup on a chain. Look out for the curious belfry, which is entirely separate from the church, having been built in the field up behind the church so the villagers could hear the bells.

Kirkoswald is a very pretty village with three pubs clustered round the cobbled market square. One of them takes its name from the Fetherstonhaugh family, which has been associated with the village since 1590.

KIRKOSWALD TO BRAMPTON

Climbing out of the village, the B6413 bears right at a junction (*Croglin, Renwick* and *Brampton*), but the route goes straight ahead, on to the minor road signed *Armathwaite* and *Carlisle*. Once past the Methodist church and some uninspiring council houses, there is a lovely view over the fields to Skiddaw and Blencathra.

Entering Staffield, go left at the T-junction (*Nunnery, Armathwaite* and *Carlisle*), past Staffield Hall Farm. The road winds through the trees, over Croglin Beck and uphill to the Nunnery House Hotel.

If you park at the hotel and pay a small fee you can get access to Nunnery Walks, a delightful, easy stroll down to the Eden Gorge and Croglin Beck Waterfall. The walks were created in the 1700s, when it was fashionable to rearrange the landscape for romantic effect.

Continue past the hotel and at the next road junction carry straight on (*Ainstable* and *Carlisle*). After another half-mile or so you emerge from the trees and can see the long ridge of the northern Pennines.

After two and a half miles, you come to a junction by Armathwaite Methodist church. Turn right (*Ainstable, Croglin, Newbiggin* and *Brampton*) and then, after a few hundred yards, go left for *Holmwrangle* and *Brampton*. After gradually climbing for half a mile you can see the Eden, snaking across the fields, and a viaduct carrying the Settle–Carlisle line. After a short climb, the road winds downhill for just over a mile to another junction. Turn left for *Cumwhitton, Castle Carrock* and *Carlisle*.

This is a good, swift minor road, winding through farmland, with super views to the Pennines. Eventually, after four miles, you come to another junction; follow the road round to the right to a

T-junction. Go left (*Castle Carrock* and *Brampton*) and into Castle Carrock.

The village itself probably won't detain you for long, but if you fancy a walk in the wilds, take the turning on the right for *Geltsdale*, just before St Peter's church. This is a long, secluded valley tucked into the flanks of the Pennines. There are one or two places where you can pull over and take a walk down to the river, and on the way back there is a tantalizing glimpse of Criffel, 38 miles away.

If you prefer a more civilized stroll, continue out of Castle Carrock for another two miles to Talkin Tarn, a large, pleasant country park. Just beyond Talkin Tarn, you come to the railway line and pass Brampton Fell signal box shortly before entering Brampton. Go straight on at the crossroads and the road takes you into Market Place, in the centre of town. You can stop

Opposite: St Oswald's Church, Kirkoswald.
Right: Priest's Walk leads from the church towards the old college, which – since 1590 – has been the home of the Fetherstonhaugh family.

here, but there is a better car-park further down the main street.

BRAMPTON TO HADRIAN'S WALL

Market Place is pretty, though rather spoilt by the rows of modern shops. The octagonal building containing the tourist information centre is the Moot Hall, built in 1817. Look out for the stocks and a bull baiting ring next to the steps. One notable visitor to Brampton was Bonnie Prince Charles, who passed through in 1745.

Follow the road through Market Place, along the main street, to St Martin's church, and turn right at the T-junction (*Hexham*). If you get the chance, have a look inside the church at the Pre-Raphaelite stained glass.

As you leave town, take the left turning at the three-forked road junction (*Lanercost Priory*, *Hadrian's Wall* and *Banks Turret*). After a couple of miles, you pass a turning for Naworth Castle, the home of the Earl of Carlisle.

A quarter of a mile after Naworth, you come to Lanercost Priory. It was founded in 1166 but has suffered over the centuries from being so near the Border. It was sacked by the Scots, occupied by passing armies (Edward I stayed here three times), and partly demolished during the Dissolution of the Monasteries. The Victorians further spoilt it by converting the nave into the parish church. It is now a rather grand old ruin in pleasant, open parkland.

The road skirts the park and you get a good view of the Priory across the field. Follow the signs for *Hadrian's Wall*, *Banks Turret* and *Birdoswald*, and the road begins to climb. Within a mile you can see the Pennines.

As you drive along you may notice a low, reddish stone wall on the right-hand side of the road. At the lay-by, pull in and have a look; that insignificant-looking structure was built almost two thousand years ago by the Emperor Hadrian.

HADRIAN'S WALL

At this point, Hadrian's Wall is six or seven feet thick but only a couple of feet high. If you follow the stones back along the road, you come to the remains of Banks Turret East.

There were small forts, or milecastles, all along the Wall, at intervals of one Roman mile (about 0.9 of a modern mile). At equal intervals between the milecastles were two turrets. Today the milecastles are numbered east to west and the turrets given letters. Banks Turret East is number 52A, so the next turret west was 52B. Not all the sites remain, so the numbers can seem a bit confusing – it's easy to think you've missed one somewhere.

At the other end of the lay-by there is a footpath through the field to Pike Hill Tower. This is a signalling site which predates the Wall; notice how the layout is at a 45-degree angle. The turret was

largely destroyed when the Victorians put the road through in 1870.

You can see why this was chosen for signalling – the view to the south is tremendous. You can see across the River Irthing and the A69 to the northern expanse of the Pennines, with Blencathra and the Lakeland fells slightly to the right. The village on the outer side of the river is Low Row.

By now you have crossed the line of the Wall, and as you drive alongside it, the next two turrets are on the left of the road. Lea Hill Turret (51B) is half a mile from Banks East, just beyond Lea Hill Farm. There is no lay-by, so pull into the side of the road to examine it. It is a small, square enclosure, with walls about three feet high. Other than a small information panel and an artist's impression, there's not a lot to see but take the opportunity to cast your eyes north. Is it imagination or does the landscape seem to be wilder, more barbarian? Those rough moorland fields could hide a whole army of Celts.

Piper Sike (51A) is a quarter of a mile further on and very easy to miss – there is not a lot here apart from foundations.

This stretch of road is rarely busy and most days you have it to yourself. Even travelling by car, there's a tremendous feeling of historical perspective as you follow the Wall; certain aspects of the view have probably changed very little in the last 1800 years.

After another mile and a half, you come to a large farm. It stands in the north-west corner of Banna Fort (sometimes marked on maps as Camboglanna), now known as Birdoswald. One of the main forts on the Wall, it was built to guard the Roman bridge over the River Irthing. It is a fascinating site, covering over five acres, and you can trace the recently excavated foundations of the fort. There is a small visitor centre, museum and shop in one of the barns.

Past Birdoswald, the road bears sharp left and the Wall marches off across the fields to the east. To follow it any further you have to walk. There is a footpath which rejoins the tour in a mile, so you could drop off any enthusiasts and pick them up later.

BIRDOSWALD TO GILSLAND
Continue to a T-junction and go right (*Gilsland* and *Greenhead*), on to the B6318. Just over half a mile from the junction, you pass a house called The Hill on your left; this is where you pick up any passengers abandoned at Birdoswald.

Whilst you're drumming your fingers on the steering wheel, look ahead and you can see a picturesque farmhouse, perched on a small promontory overlooking the river gorge. It is on the site of another turret, Willowford, at the point where the Wall crossed the River Irthing.

Approaching Gilsland, keep to the main road (*Gilsland* and *Greenhead*), over a bridge and into the village. As you pass a lorry park on your left, the B6318 goes left (*Greenhead*) but the road appears to go round to the right. If you take the wrong turning, use it as an

opportunity to look at Willowford before coming back to the B6318.

As you go through the centre of Gilsland, look out for the signs for *Poltross Burn Mile Castle* (number 48), one of the most interesting milecastles along the Wall. It is down a narrow lane on the right, just after you pass under the railway bridge. Park by the Station Hotel and walk across.

On leaving the village, follow the signs for *Hexham* (ignoring the turning for Greenhead and the museum at Carvoran Roman fort), and this brings you to the A69.

GILSLAND TO LAMBLEY
By turning left on to the A69 (*Hexham*, *Corebridge* and *Newcastle*) you now plunge briefly into Northumberland. The landscape ahead and to the left shows some curious features – great wedge-shaped escarpments caused by older, tougher igneous rocks thrusting through to the surface.

The road runs alongside the Carlisle to Newcastle railway line for two and a half miles. As it bears away from the line and you enter Haltwhistle, take the turning to the right (*Alston* and *Whitfield*) on to a minor road which crosses the South Tyne River via a single-track bridge. At the T-junction, shortly afterwards, go right (*Featherstone Park*, *Coanwood* and *Alston*), and this will take you through pleasant, open countryside and up the lower slopes of Plenmeller Common. You get the impression someone has really tried hard to come up with picturesque names. It is delightful countryside, all the more attractive for the fact that hardly any visitors from the central Lakes and Dales bother to find their way out here.

As the road climbs you get a good view into Border country on the left and of the long, low ridge of Byers Pike ahead. Keep following the signs for *Featherstone*, *Coanwood* and *Alston*, through Park village. A mile beyond the village, Featherstone Park is signed off to your right. Ignore the turning and continue along the main road, passing one or two more houses at Rowfoot, and climbing quite

steeply for a while. Byers Pike and Glendue Fell dominate the view.

Keep following the signs for Alston. The road rises and drops, twisting around the folds of the hills and turns back on itself as you pass Coanwood. You start a steep descent into a river valley. After a long left-hand bend, which takes in the bridge over the South Tyne River, you climb back on to your original heading.

Follow the road for another three-quarters of a mile, past the turning for Lambley, and you come to the T-junction with the A689. Turn left for the bustling market town of *Alston*.

LAMBLEY TO ALSTON
This must be one of the wildest and most secluded A roads in the country. In winter it can be bleak, but travel along here on a warm autumn afternoon and the colours are fantastic. The road runs above the South Tyne river valley, following the contours of the hill, and the fells contain a wonderful array of rich colours.

Just over a mile along the A689, the road crosses Glendue Burn. Notice the use of the Scots word for stream; until Edward I intervened in the thirteenth century, all this land belonged to Scotland. As you weave around the folds of Glendue Fell, you are travelling just below the course of the Maiden Way, the Roman road which ran from the junction of routes at Hadrian's Wall to Appleby.

This side of the valley is quite rough and desolate, in sharp contrast with the lush pasture over to the east. You pass through the teeming metropolis of Slaggyford and three miles later enter Cumbria. Ahead, you can just see Alston, ringed by fells. You eventually arrive at a T-junction, beside a war memorial. The signpost opposite reads *Penrith* right, *Town Centre*, *Barnard Castle* and *Durham* left. The latter seems strangely

displaced in the middle of a tour which started on the fringes of the Lake District.

Turn left and follow the road over the bridge into Alston. The town centre is up the cobbled road on the right, but to park continue downhill to the large car-park by the petrol station.

ALSTON

Alston is the highest market town in England (1,000ft above sea level) and one of the most remote – almost 20 miles from the nearest town. It was the market town for the surrounding communities of Nenthead, Leadgate and Garrigill, and stands at the crossroads of five major routes. The hills around Alston are rich in lead, silver and zinc and have been mined since the thirteenth century. It really boomed in the 1800s when the London Mining Company built the network of 'all-weather roads' that converge at Alston. There is still plenty of evidence

of the industry – especially at Nenthead – but mining gradually declined in the late nineteenth century, largely owing to foreign competition.

Alston's steep, cobbled main street is quite attractive, as is the covered Market Cross, but on the whole there is a slightly odd feel to the place. As you look around, you realize where all the hippies went at the end of the 1960s. And what is the Arthurian connection? There is a shop called Camelot Carpets and another, even weirder one, called the King Arthur Bottle Specialist. However, it has its more conventional attractions; go down the lane behind the cross and you come to Gossipgate Galleries, a neat contemporary gallery, specializing in crafts and paintings.

ALSTON TO HARTSIDE

Go back to the junction by the war memorial and carry straight on (*Pen-*

rith). This is another typical Cumbrian A road, lined by drystone walls, winding about and climbing steadily. Across the moor to the left, beyond another ridge, is Ash Gill waterfall. It is visible just as you pass the turning for Leadgate and Garrigill, and you may also be lucky enough to catch a glimpse of Black Burn.

After six miles of windswept moor, you come to Hartside Top, 1,940ft above sea level. There is a small café and car-park, and if you pull in by the low stone wall, you don't even have to leave your car for one of the finest panoramas in England.

You look west, across the patchwork quilt of the Eden valley to Penrith and the Lakeland fells. High Street is just left of Penrith, leading your eye south to Harter Fell and Shap. Just right of the town are Blencathra and Skiddaw, and then you can look across to the Solway Firth,

*The remains of Poltross Burn, Milecastle 48, Gilsland,
one of the best preserved milecastles. At this point
the walkway along the top of the Wall was
about eleven feet high.*

Criffel and the Galloway Hills. If you want to examine the view more closely, there is a coin-operated pair of binoculars mounted on a pillar by the wall.

The tea-room is one of England's highest 'transport caffs', but is otherwise unremarkable.

HARTSIDE TO PENRITH

A very steep descent takes you down a series of long switchbacks with wonderful and highly distracting views. After three miles you come back into lovely green countryside, a refreshing change after the moor, and drop into Melmerby village. In a distance of a little under five miles – from Hartside Top – you have descended 1,400ft.

At the initial planning stages of this book, it became apparent that at least five of the fifteen tours seemed to take a detour through Melmerby. Go to the Village Bakery and you'll see why. In addition to making and selling their own bread – all baked in a wood-fired oven – they also run a wonderful café. All their produce is organically grown, some of it is even home-grown, and the flour comes from the mill at Little Salkeld. The wonderful bakery stands in the group of houses to your right, above Melmerby's magnificent thirteen-acre village green.

Suitably stuffed, waddle back to the car and set off again for Penrith. Leaving the village, you pass groups of trees designed to act as breaks for the notorious Helm Wind, the only wind in the country with its own name. When the cold north-easterly winds blow in late winter and spring, the shape of Cross Fell, and the local atmospheric conditions just above the ridge, combine to create a harsh, dry wind which locals claim can 'blow t'nebs off t'geese'. 'Nebs' are beaks, by the way.

The road leads through Langwathby to the iron road bridge over the Eden and back to Penrith.

You feel a real sense of discovery when exploring the borders of Cumbria and Northumberland, and although this is not the longest tour in the book – in terms of miles – you'd be advised to set out prepared for a long day. The route follows the River Eden for much of the way and then heads north into Border territory.

Once at Brampton, you could – if pressed for time – follow the main road straight to Alston, but Hadrian's Wall really shouldn't be missed; it has a real sense of drama about it. It was built in 122 AD, and was manned for over 250 years by a regular garrison of 13,000 men, mostly recruited from the local population. It stretched 73 miles (80 Roman miles), from Wallsend, at Newcastle, to Bowness-on-Solway. More than a million cubic yards of stone went into the construction of the wall and associated forts. Once it was abandoned, much of the brickwork was raided for local buildings. There are a number of exhibitions and museums devoted to Hadrian's Wall – you pass one at Birdoswald and there is another, a short detour away, at Carvoran. Look out for all the old cast-iron sign posts bearing names like Brampton Junction and Haltwhistle. They could have come straight from a Rowland Emmett railway cartoon. Haltwhistle was once linked to Alston via a branch line, opened by the Newcastle and Carlisle Railway Company in 1852. When British Rail closed it in 1976, a preservation society was formed which now runs steam trains on part of the line.

The area around Alston can be cut off in winter, with snow drifts of up to fifteen feet deep. Look out for the snow poles by the roadside, as you head down Hartside. Hartside has one of the most spectacular views in the book, and is especially welcome after the long haul along the back of the Pennines.

Hadrian's Wall.

TOUR NINE
~
The Villages of the Eden

Falling between the Lakeland fells and the
Pennines, the Eden Valley is largely
ignored by the majority of tourists, and
they are missing an absolute gem. This
tour explores the south Eden, a quiet,
rural district with winding country lanes,
delightful scenery and a rich and
fascinating history.

Appleby-in-Westmorland and Great Asby, to Crosby
Ravensworth, Maulds Meaburn, Kings Meaburn and
Morland, back via Askham, Eamont Bridge and Brougham
Castle.
Distance: 50 miles. Driving time: 2½–3 hours

*Early morning at Meyburgh Henge,
near Eamont Bridge, Penrith.*

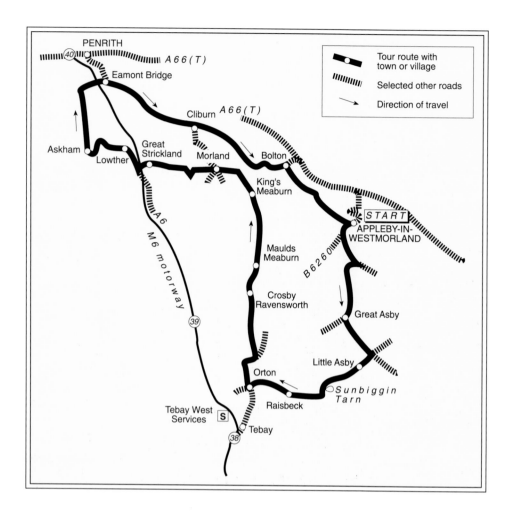

Below: High Cross in Boroughgate, Appleby. In addition to marking the limits of the old market place, it also serves as a sun dial. Opposite: The Eden Valley from Cross Fell.

APPLEBY TO GREAT ASBY

The tour begins in Appleby, at the Moot Hall in Boroughgate. Drive up the street towards Appleby Castle and follow the road round to the right.

The town became Appleby-in-Westmorland in 1974, more or less as an act of defiance at the local government boundary changes which merged Cumberland and Westmorland into the new county of Cumbria.

It is a very ancient town. The Normans established a defensive settlement here, on a loop in the River Eden, and built the castle and church, probably between 1100 and 1120 (although both have later additions). The entrances to Boroughgate are typically Norman – narrow and easily defended against the persistent raids from the north. It worked for over two hundred years, until the Scots virtually destroyed the town in 1388.

Boroughgate is a wide, attractive main street which runs from the castle down to the church of St Lawrence. The street is bordered by lime trees, planted by the bell-ringers of St Lawrence in 1876. High and Low Cross, the white and black pillars at the top and bottom of Boroughgate, mark the limits of the market-place. Just above Low Cross is the sixteenth-century Moot Hall (which contains the tourist information centre). A 'moot', or 'mote', was a meeting where the town burghers used to assemble to transact business.

Appleby Castle still has a Norman keep and Great Hall, but the main fabric of the building was rebuilt by Lady Anne Clifford in 1653. The castle and earthworks are open to the public, and are worth visiting just for the superb view over the town from the tower. As you pass the castle and head downhill, you may notice that whoever spelt the street name appears to have changed his or her mind about 'i before e' before reaching the bottom of the street.

Now the road climbs out of town, and you stay on the B6260, heading for Orton. After half a mile, you will come to a sign for *Ormside, Great Asby* and *Soulby*. Turn left here, on to a minor road. You get a superb view across to the Pennines on your left.

After another mile, take the turning on the right for *Great Asby*. This is quite a wide, minor road which meanders through pleasant, pastoral scenery. A mile down this road you will pass a sign for Rutter Force, where a short walk will bring you to a small waterfall on Hoff Beck.

Eventually, after three and a half miles, you come to a crossroads. The road to the left (*Lower Asby, Soulby* and *Kirkby Stephen*) skirts Great Asby and continues to head south. However, if you carry straight on, you come into the attractive little village.

Go past the Victorian church, with its slate-covered lychgate, and turn left, over the beck. Left again takes you back along the other side of the church and past the Three Greyhounds pub. This minor diversion was designed solely to show you the three concrete greyhounds mounted on the wall by the pub. Follow the road round to the right and you are back on the tour.

GREAT ASBY TO ORTON

The countryside around here is very reminiscent of the Yorkshire Dales, with neat farms and patterns of fields, criss-crossed by white limestone walls. As you climb, the views to your left – to Dufton Fell and the northern Pennines – are simply spectacular. You get an excellent view of Ingleborough, directly ahead of you.

Two and a half miles from Great Asby, take the turning on the right for *Little Asby, Newbiggin* and *Orton*. This takes you up on to a limestone escarpment and past the turning for Little Asby. The name is accurate, for this is a tiny hamlet stuck out on the moor which may once, in medieval times, have had a sanctuary for lepers.

As you drop down the other side of the escarpment you have a terrific view of the Howgills, to your left, and the Shap Fells, directly ahead. Continuing past the turning for Newbiggin and Ravenstonedale, you come upon Sunbiggin Tarn tucked into a fold in the hillside, directly below you. This spot is very popular with bird-watchers, as thousands of black-headed gulls nest here in early summer. If you feel an urge to stretch your legs, avoid the fields around the tarn – they can be very boggy and dangerous.

When driving along this stretch of road the view across the moor is extremely distracting, for the Howgills are spectacular from this angle, especially if lit by a good sunset. Meanwhile watch out for cows wandering across the road – they have no more traffic sense than sheep.

As you come down off the moor you arrive at a T-junction. Go right (*Orton*) and past the tiny hamlet of Raisbeck. The distinctive limestone scar on the right is Great Asby Scar. Keep following the road, and a mile and a half beyond Raisbeck you approach a group of houses and come to a T-junction on the outskirts of Orton. Go right (*Shap* and *Appleby*) and into Orton.

ORTON TO KING'S MEABURN

There are several attractive houses in Orton, which makes up for the fact that the village centre seems to consist of a large car parking area and a public convenience. Look out for the aeroplane weathervanes in the garden opposite the George Hotel.

Ignore the turning to Shap and keep to the main road. As you leave the village the road weaves its way across a long, low fell and then begins to climb Orton Scar. As the road levels off and goes over a cattle grid, take the turning on the left for *Crosby Ravensworth*. This is a minor road, but the verge either side gives plenty of room to pass oncoming traffic. After two and a half miles, you cross Lyvennet Beck via a small, humpbacked bridge and shortly afterwards you come into Crosby Ravensworth.

Jennywell Hall, on your left as you enter the village, is an impressive old building, now an antique shop. Once again ignore the turning for Shap, and keep straight on until you come to St Lawrence's church. This is worth a closer look; it is set back from the road and the only way you can approach it is via a little humpbacked footbridge over the beck. The church is an impressive red stone building and has a wonderful clocktower with gargoyles at the top and a funny little spire in one corner. The church was largely restored in the early nineteenth century but the arched doorway dates from 1240.

As you leave the village you pass Weston House – which you can't miss

as it is bright pink – and within a quarter of a mile you are entering Maulds Meaburn. This is another very attractive village. The road drops down from the fell and you enter the village overlooking the Lyvennet and the small cluster of houses. You come level with the river and the village green (watch out for sheep), passing the first two bridges and turnings for Appleby and Holesfoot. Keep going until the road bears left, just by the seventeenth-century Meaburn Hall, and then turn right, over another bridge (*King's Meaburn*).

This is prosperous farming country, so expect to encounter large Volvo estate cars. After two miles or so, you come into King's Meaburn. This is a neat village rather than a pretty one. The name means just what it says: it was one half of the old manor of Meaburn, once owned by Hugh de Morville. When he was implicated in the murder of Thomas à Becket, Hugh's half was seized by the crown. The other half was owned by his sister, Maud – hence the modern name Maulds Meaburn.

KING'S MEABURN TO ASKHAM

One of the beauties of this route is the perspective it gives you of the mountains on either side of the Eden valley. Look right as you leave the village and there is a tremendous sense of distance, rare in the central Lakes, as you gaze across the pattern of fields to Cross Fell and Alston Moor.

A mile beyond King's Meaburn, take the turning on the left for *Morland* and *Shap*. It is easy to miss the sign, so watch out for it. This is a sharp hairpin bend and the road drops down to cross the Lyvennet via a narrow sandstone bridge. The river is very wide and meandering at this point and amuses itself with a few extravagant loops across the fields.

This pleasant country lane brings you into Morland. Keep on the main road, ignoring the turning to the left as you come into the village, and you cross a small bridge to arrive at the Crown Inn and, just opposite, is a telephone box and a small lay-by.

Examples of the attractive houses along Askham's main street. The village was once part of the Lowther estate and there have been settlements in the area since the late Stone Age.

As you travel about the Lake District, you get used to all the shops selling outdoor equipment and wet weather gear, but Morland used to have one of the most specialized. The Survival Aids Shop had distinctly military overtones – NATO issue water bottles, collapsible heliographs, survival knives, inflatable camouflage trousers . . . Despite the fact that they now have branches all over the country, the original shop closed in 1993. Perhaps even the most adventurous outdoor type found it too far from civilization.

Continue up the main street, turn right at the top of the hill, signed *Cliburn* and *Penrith*, and then take the next left (*Great Strickland*). Before you make the turning, you might want to park and have a look at the church, with its eleventh-century tower.

In less than half a mile you have climbed out of the village and are in open countryside once more. It's hard to believe that in the Middle Ages Morland was Westmorland's third largest settlement, second only to Appleby and Kendal.

Once through Great Strickland you may spot lorries trundling across the skyline ahead of you. The road passes under the main Lancaster to Carlisle railway line and brings you to a T-junction with the A6. This wide main road comes as something of a shock after the narrow lanes and byways between here and Appleby. Take a deep breath and turn right (*Penrith, Hackthorpe* and *Clifton*). In fact, the chances are that the road will not be busy; most of the heavy traffic thunders along the M6, which you drive over almost immediately afterwards.

Hackthorpe village is tiny. Don't put your foot down or you'll miss the next turning. About three hundred yards past the Lowther Castle Inn, turn left (*Lowther*) and you are back on a narrow country lane. Take the next left (*Lowther*), which appears to take you

through a private housing estate, although you are still on a public highway. Continue past the entrance to the Lakeland Bird of Prey Centre, then the road bears round to the right, past another row of cottages. These are all part of the Lowther Estate. To the left of you at this point there is a rich and attractive park dotted with trees. This is all private land, so if you feel the urge to stop and walk, keep to the public footpaths.

Follow the signs for *Askham* and the road takes you downhill, through the park. Keep glancing left and you suddenly see the most amazing Gothic castle, standing on a hill at the end of a long avenue of oak trees. It is totally unexpected, totally out of place and totally fake.

The Lowther family have owned this estate for over seven hundred years. The first Lowther Hall was built some time in

the thirteenth century, but was burnt down in the 1720s. The present Lowther Castle was constructed in 1811, but by 1936 it was proving too expensive to maintain, so the family moved to Askham Hall and most of the building was demolished, leaving only this impressive facade. It looks as though it might have been a try-out for Euro Disney which went wrong.

As you start to leave the park, the little church on your right is St Michael's. Partly thirteenth-century but mostly Victorian, it stands in a commanding position, overlooking the River Lowther. In the churchyard is Lowther mausoleum. It's worth stopping to have a look. Look out for the strange stones in the church porch; these are Norse gravestones, over a thousand years old.

The road drops down to the river and over a pretty red sandstone bridge before climbing again, past St Peter's church. It

takes you up through the centre of Askham village. This is a very pretty spot, one of the loveliest villages in Cumbria. The broad main street is lined with trees and grassy banks. The name means 'the place with the ash trees'. As you drive up from the bridge, the big house on your right is Askham Hall. The Hall is not open to the public, unfortunately, but you get glimpses of it from the public footpath alongside.

ASKHAM TO EAMONT BRIDGE

At the top of the village, just by the village shop, turn right (*Yanwath* and *Penrith*). As you make the turning, there is a cul-de-sac on the left which is a good place to park if you want to have a wander about in the village.

The main road leads you out of the village into open countryside again. After a short distance there is a good view of the northern Pennines on your right and you

The keep, Brougham Castle. This is the oldest part of the building, built by Robert de Vipont in the reign of Henry II. The second floor originally provided accommodation for the lord's family.

bridge and then you want to turn left for *Brougham Castle* and *Brough*, on to another B road. This goes under a small bridge and you find yourself driving alongside a high wall on your right. This is the boundary of Brougham Hall.

Brougham (pronounced 'broom') is a corruption of Brocavum, the name of the Roman fort just to the east. The Hall was, from 1868, the home of Lord Brougham and Vaux, Lord Chancellor of England and the designer of the Brougham carriage. He was also the model for the Lord Chancellor in Gilbert and Sullivan's *Iolanthe*.

In 1726 the Hall was sold for £5,000. In 1934 its value had dropped to £290. It was sold again in 1948 for £7,700 and then, in 1986, it was given to the Brougham Hall Trust for the sum of one peppercorn.

The Hall itself is largely a ruin but is being restored to provide a centre for local trades and crafts. Entrance to the public is free, though they suggest a small donation. If you peer through the doorway you will see, just past the guardhouse on the right, a door bearing the most appalling pun – Brougham Cupboard.

Continue past the Hall, ignoring the turnings for Clifton and Shap. The Pennines put in another appearance ahead of you as you start to climb slightly. Three-quarters of a mile from Brougham Hall you arrive at a small crossroads, signed *Brougham Castle* left, *Wetheriggs Pottery* right. Go left, down a narrow lane. You can already see the castle, a magnificent ruin which towers above the trees on your left. You'll find a cul-de-sac on your right, just opposite the castle, where you can park if you want to explore.

Brougham is probably the most interesting ruined castle in Cumbria. The keep stands four storeys high and you can climb to the tiny, vaulted chapel at the top and get an excellent view of the surround-

can look down across the plain to Penrith. Relax and enjoy the superb, long, slow descent to the main road.

Arriving at the T-junction with the B5320, two and a half miles from Askham, turn right (*Eamont Bridge* and *Penrith*). The road goes over the railway line and half a mile afterwards, just as you cross the River Eamont, there is a sign for *Mayburgh Henge* and *Southwaite Green*. Turn left here for a short detour to one of Cumbria's most sombre and mysterious prehistoric monuments.

Mayburgh Henge is a short distance down the lane, on your right. Park by the road, walk through the kissing gate and climb the steep, grassy embankment. Once at the top, you will realize that you are standing on a 15ft high circular bank, over 1,500ft across. In the centre stands a solitary stone, nine ft high. It is all that is left of two concentric stone circles which once stood here. The bank is built

of stones, though now overgrown with grass and topped with trees. This site is somewhere between three and four thousand years old and was probably a Neolithic meeting-place. It has a very dark, brooding air to it.

Go back on to the B5320 and continue towards Eamont Bridge. Just as the road reaches the A6, there is another prehistoric monument on your right. This is known as Arthur's Round Table, which is a complete misnomer as it dates from the same period as Mayburgh Henge. There is not a lot to see here – just a wide ditch and an earthen bank. A large part of it was destroyed when the road was brought through. The cross, just by the junction, is a monument to two local men who died in the Boer War.

EAMONT BRIDGE AND BROUGHAM
At the junction, go right (*Kendal, Brough* and *Lowther Park*). The road goes over a

ing countryside. The keep is the oldest part, built sometime in the early thirteenth century. It became the family seat of the Cliffords, who added and improved the castle right up until the last of the line, Lady Anne Clifford, died here in 1676. After her death, the castle passed to the Earls of Thanet, who preferred to live at Appleby Castle. Brougham was partly demolished in 1691.

It is still an impressive structure, and overlooks the fields where the Roman fort of Brocavum once stood. The castle is open to the public and now in the care of English Heritage.

BROUGHAM TO APPLEBY

From the car-park, return to the cross-roads and go straight across (*Wetheriggs Pottery*). Follow this narrow lane for a mile and a quarter to a T-junction. Go left (*Wetheriggs Pottery, Cliburn* and *Bolton*), on to another minor road, from which there are more good views across the plain to the Pennine hills. You pass through the small hamlet of Clifton Dykes and come to Wetheriggs Steam Pottery on your right. By now you must be ready for a tea stop, and the pottery has a café and shop attached.

You continue along this wide, straight minor road for another three and a half miles. The views are excellent and this stretch is a thoroughly enjoyable drive. It eventually brings you into the red sandstone village of Bolton. Turn right (*Colby*), just opposite the New Crown Inn. As you leave the village, there is a lovely view left to Burney Hill, Knock Pike and Dufton Pike, the three conical hills which lie at the foot of the Pennines. After another two miles you enter the village of Colby, which is tiny – if you are not careful, you're out again almost before you know it.

The road climbs again and just before you drop into the outskirts of Appleby you get a wonderful view of the Pennines, looking across the rooftops, with Appleby Castle in the middle distance. You descend to a T-junction and go left, back into Boroughgate via Shaw's Weind (or Wiend) and the intriguingly-named Doomsgate.

I was brought up in Bray, near Maidenhead, which is a very picturesque place, and I have always liked scenic villages and quaint hamlets. The Eden valley has a wealth of them – clean, attractive, charming and, moreover, most of them are living, thriving communities. It also has very pretty, rather gentle countryside which is quite a contrast to the rugged fells and mountains to be found on either side.

Brougham Hall is a place which rarely crops up on an itinerary of places to visit. It is not really a tourist attraction in itself, though it does house some fascinating craft workshops, and has some intriguing motoring connections. The Brougham carriage was invented here, in 1831. It was designed to carry two passengers and had a modern, elliptically-sprung suspension. It was drawn by a single horse and the driver sat outside; when passengers wanted to give directions they attracted his attention by pulling a cord attached to a button on his coat. An early motorized version established a land-speed record in 1899. Powered by electric batteries it reached 60 mph over a standing mile. The Brougham has gone on to give its name to top-of-the-range cars produced in the United States by General Motors and Ford.

Brougham Hall was the scene of another historic event in October 1905, when Edward VII became the first English monarch to drive a car through Cumbria. His 20 bhp, plum-coloured Mercedes was driven down from Balmoral and then the king drove across the Pennines to County Durham and back. He was accompanied by six other cars in case he broke down. The entire road was hand-swept, so he wouldn't get a puncture, and there were policemen at every intersection in case he lost his way.

Finally, take the time to explore Brougham Castle, one of the most impressive ruins in the country.

Brougham Castle, near Penrith.

TOUR TEN
~
Richmond and Swaledale

No description, however well written, can quite prepare the first-time visitor to Richmond. It stands above the entrance to Swaledale, a majestic gateway to one of the best-loved valleys in the Yorkshire Dales. This tour explores the length of Swaledale and Arkengarthdale, linking them with a trip to the highest pub in England.

From Richmond and Reeth, along Swaledale to Muker, then up West Stones Dale to the Tan Hill Inn and back via Arkengarthdale.
Distance: 49 miles. Driving time: 2 hours

Field barns at Cloggerby Rigg,
Upper Swaledale.

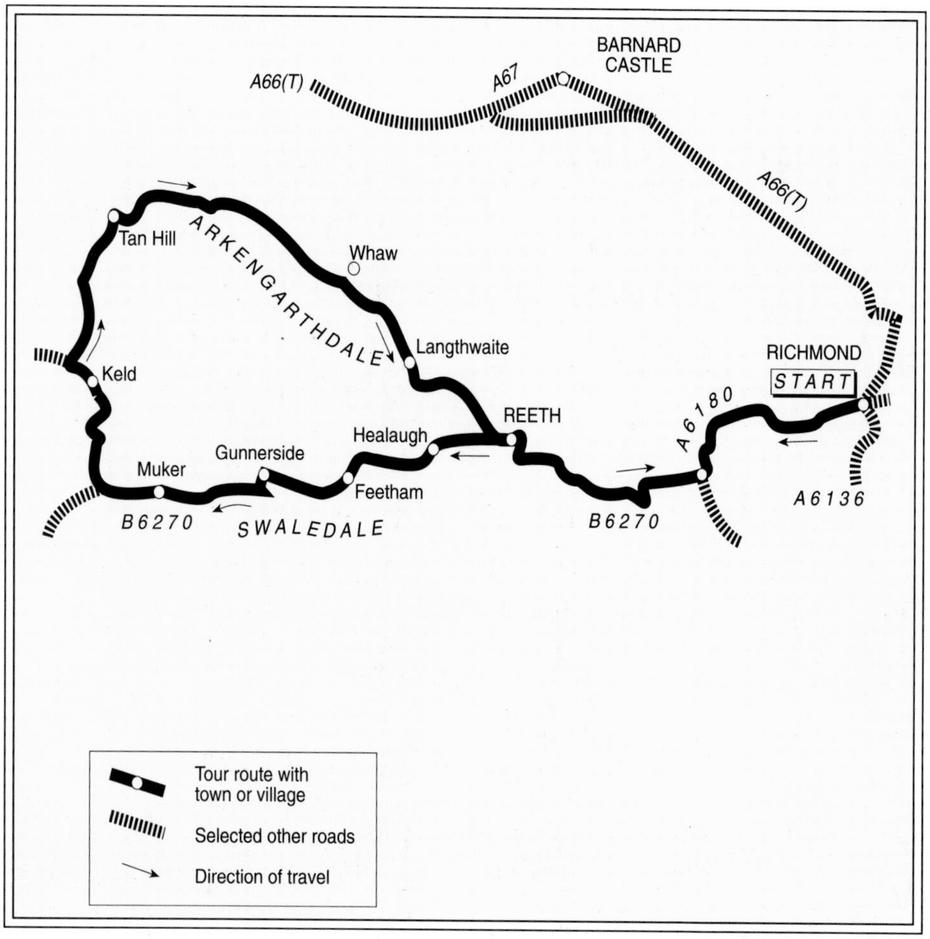
BARNARD CASTLE
A66(T)
A67
A66(T)
Tan Hill
ARKENGARTHDALE
Whaw
Langthwaite
Keld
RICHMOND
START
A6180
REETH
Healaugh
Gunnerside
Muker
Feetham
A6136
B6270
SWALEDALE
B6270
Tour route with town or village
Selected other roads
Direction of travel

The magnificent view from the keep of Richmond Castle, looking west into Swaledale. Culloden Tower, in the distance, was built in 1746 to mark the defeat of Bonnie Prince Charlie.

Richmond

Richmond has a very French feel to it. A series of narrow, ancient streets, or 'wynds', radiate downhill from Market Place, the wide, open, cobbled centre of town.

At the top of Market Place is an unusual eighteenth-century market 'cross', or, to be exact, an octagonal pillar topped with a stone ball. In front of it, right in the centre of the square, is Holy Trinity church, built around 1135 (though rebuilt a couple of times since) and possibly the only church in the country with shops built into its aisles. It is no longer a place of worship and now houses the Regimental Museum of the Green Howards.

From the market cross, you can't miss Richmond Castle, towering above the shops. You can get to it via the little passageway, to the left of the Bishop Blaize Inn (named, apparently, after the Patron Saint of Armenia and Saint of Sore Throats!).

The castle was built in 1071 by Alan Rufus, Earl of Brittany, whose father fought alongside William the Conqueror at Hastings. There are only two other stone castles as old as this in the whole country, at Durham and Colchester. The castle is in the care of English Heritage and open to the public, which means you can investigate the amazing twelfth-century keep; 100ft high with walls almost eleven ft thick. At the base is an archway which is probably all that remains of the original eleventh-century castle.

Richmond to Reeth

Leave Market Place via King Street, just to the left of the King's Head Hotel, and at the roundabout go left, signed *Leyburn* and *Reeth.* As you turn into Victoria Road, the tourist information centre is on your right. Just behind it is Grey Friar's Tower, the remains of a medieval Franciscan friary. Look right and you will spot the Georgian Theatre, the oldest theatre in the UK, built by Samuel Butler in 1788. It fell into disuse in the 1840s but was reopened after a lengthy restoration in 1963. Book early – it only seats 240.

Within a mile of leaving Richmond you are out in the countryside, driving along the thickly wooded valley of the River Swale. As the road crosses the river, you enter the Yorkshire Dales National Park. The long, limestone escarpment on your right is Whitcliffe Scar.

This is a good country A road, with plenty of views and enough charm and interest to keep drivers and passengers amused. There are lovely, intermittent views of the river, and just before you enter a pleasant avenue of trees, you pass a distinctive brown crag on your left.

A quarter of a mile farther on, take the turning on the right, signed *Reeth, B6270,* to keep following the river valley. This road, still known as New Road, was built as a turnpike in 1836. The original road ran north of here, along the fell through Marske and Fremington.

After driving along the B road for a mile and a half, you cross Gill Beck and the road swings right in an extravagant curve; the view is quite restricted at this point but you can see another limestone band above Scar Spring Wood, on your left. The escarpment is at the northern edge of Stainton Moor, now used largely as a military firing range by troops stationed at Catterick.

Keep a look-out for Abbey Farm and you may spot a ruined tower behind it; this is all that remains of Ellerton Priory, sacked by Scots raiders in 1342. As you drive into Swaledale, the view becomes a marvellous chequer-board of fields, laced with white drystone walls, with Calver Hill as a backdrop.

Passing through the village of Grinton (which means 'the green pasture'), the

road bears right, over the River Swale and into Fremington. The long, limestone escarpment above the village is Fremington Edge. As you leave Fremington, bear left over another long bridge and you immediately enter Reeth.

REETH AND SWALEDALE

Reeth has a way of sneaking up on you. The first impression, as you go past the village shop, is of a fairly routine little place, but the road leads you uphill and suddenly you find that you are in the centre of a wide and attractive village green, ringed with houses. Reeth sits on the western edge of Calver Hill, actually above the Swale valley, almost on a plateau.

It is a very picturesque spot and Herriot historians will have fun identifying scenes from the films and television series. The Black Bull pub appeared in *It Shouldn't Happen to a Vet*, the second

of the Herriot feature films. The corner house of the terrace, opposite the Buck Hotel, was used as Siegfried Farnon's surgery. The Buck Hotel and some of the shops were used in the BBC television series.

The Swaledale Museum is off to the right of the main road. By the Buck Hotel is a turning to Langwith, Barnard Castle and Arkengarthdale. You will get the chance to explore that later; for now, go straight on, following the sign for *Gunnerside*, *Kirkby Stephen* and *Swaledale*.

As you leave the village, pause and look back at the superb view down the valley. The patterns of fields and boundaries make it look like a toy landscape. There is also a delightful view ahead, into the heart of Swaledale, the patchwork of fields sweeping down the fells to the river below. Whitaside and Brownsey Moor converge ahead of you

in a V, and the river is an absolute picture; a winding silver ribbon leading you along the dale. This is classic Dales scenery, the sort of view that keeps Mr Kodak in business.

Although the road is quite narrow at this point, there is room for two cars, which is just as well as you may want to keep pulling over to let others past as you enjoy the view. A mile or so after Reeth you will have to slow down as you pass through the hamlet of Healaugh, where the barns and houses cluster right to the edge of the narrow road.

From Healaugh, the road descends to the river and then climbs again, through Feetham and Low Row. At Low Row, the houses stand back from the road, separated by a narrow stretch of village green. Just after Low Row, you pass a turning for the wonderfully-named hamlet of Crackpot. In the thirteenth century it was known as Crakepote, and

the name probably derives from the Norse word 'kraka', for crow. Pity, really.

On the far side of the river, the fields climb the grassy ridge of Summer Lodge Moor (so called because it was the summer residence of the herdsmen who worked for the canons of Bridlington Priory). Beyond this, to the south, lie Askrigg and Wensleydale, less than four miles away as the crow flies.

A mile and a half farther on you come into Gunnerside. Just past the King's Head Hotel, follow the road to the left for *Muker* and *Kirkby Stephen*. Leaving the village the road drops down to a narrow and dramatic bridge over the River Swale. On the other side, there is a series of steep zigzags up through Hag Wood, and when you reach the top you can see across to the far side of the valley.

Half a mile before you enter the village of Muker, you part company with the Swale, which goes round the opposite side of Kisdon Fell. Muker is a tremendously neat and ordered village, looking as though it is in its Sunday best, prepared at any moment for the television cameras to pop up and film another Herriot series.

Like a number of villages in Swaledale and Arkengarthdale, Muker was once a centre for lead mining. Lead had been dug from the hills in Roman times, but the activity reached its peak in the eighteenth century when small workings scattered about the valleys employed up to 2,000 men, excavating 6,000 tons of lead ore a year. The industry declined at the end of the nineteenth century, but there is still plenty of evidence on the surrounding hills.

WEST STONESDALE AND TAN HILL
The road takes you over a couple of narrow, humpbacked bridges. On your left, Straw Beck descends in a series of pretty cascades. As you leave the village, and the road starts to climb, look left again and you may spot a tiny waterfall,

crashing down the small crag in the trees.

There is another good view ahead once you are past Thwaite and come level with Hooker Mill Scar on your right. Take the opportunity to glance at the view behind, too, before it vanishes behind the escarpment. After two miles of undulating road you come to the turning for Keld, just by a war memorial. Keld village is actually off the main route, but you can explore it by following the minor lane round two sides of a triangle and joining the B6270 again a quarter of a mile farther on. From the village there is a good walk to Kisdon Force, the waterfall half a mile or so to the east.

Once you are past the second turning for Keld the road drops abruptly and after half a mile you need to take the minor road on the right, signed *West Stonesdale* and *Tan Hill*. This takes you over the River Swale again, after which

you begin climbing in earnest (or, better, in first gear). The short, initial stretch is the most difficult; a one-in-four gradient with three hairpin bends. Then the climb eases somewhat and you may have time to admire the view. Just below the summit of the ridge on your right runs the Pennine Way.

After climbing for just over half a mile, you go over a cattle grid and find yourself with open fell on the left. Stonesdale Beck lies beyond the stone wall on your right.

Stonesdale Moor can be very bleak at times. Numerous small rivers and streams have cut through the peat to make a landscape slashed with black scars. The road carries on climbing, crossing the occasional bridge; don't take them at speed – this is not the place to lose your exhaust pipe. After a couple of miles, as you approach the top, the view opens out and it is possible to get some idea of where you are going, despite

the extravagant way in which the road winds across the moor.

After three miles of climbing, the sight of a pub, standing isolated at the top of the moor, comes as a bit of shock. This is Tan Hill Inn, at 1,732ft above sea level the highest pub in England (the second highest is in the Peak District). This isolated building, over four miles from the nearest village, owes its existence to the coal industry. Collieries of one sort or another have existed on Stonesdale Moor since the thirteenth century. At the end of the nineteenth century, fifty or sixty carts a day would call at Tan Hill to carry coal from the surrounding pits. Tan Hill Colliery was the last to be worked and closed in 1932. The Inn was originally King's Pit House, built in the eighteenth century, and was a private house until about 1916. It stands on an old turnpike road, opened in 1741, which linked Reeth and Brough.

As you approach the pub you come to a T-junction, but it's not the sort of place where you have to wait for a break in the traffic. Turn right and you arrive at this venerable landmark.

ARKENGARTHDALE

Just past the Inn, there is a wonderful view north over the black expanse of Bowes Moor and Stainmore Forest (not a tree in sight) towards the A66 and Barnard Castle. The A66 runs very straight as it follows the old Roman road. Day and night there always seem to be lorries thundering along it. It is only three and a half miles away, but from here is looks as if it is in a different world.

You are now heading almost due east, across Arkengarthdale Moor. The tall snow poles at the roadside, which indicate the line of the road, give you a clue to what conditions are like in winter. After two miles of moor you get a surprising

glimpse of colour ahead; it is the head of Arkengarthdale, a brave intrusion of rich, green fields, which draws you along the road like a magnet. The contrast is even more marked in autumn, when the moor is a mixture of delicate shades of browns and purples and the head of the valley looks impossibly green in comparison. There is even a white painted house, just at the edge of the fields.

As you approach Arkengarthdale, you begin to pick up the first of the becks feeding into Arkle Beck, which runs the length of the valley. The road drops down through rich farming land and you pass a sign for Whaw. You can see the old quarry workings above you, on the left, on Low Moor. A mile farther down you pass a series of spoil heaps – more evidence of lead mining – and come into the village of Langthwaite. There is an attractive church on your left, just down a short turning. This is the church

A quarter of a mile east of Keld, the River Swale cuts its way through the limestone terrain to create a shallow ravine and the series of cascades known as Kisdon Force.

of St Mary, and the track beside leads to the entrance to Scar House, the rather fine manor house which has been in view, on the far side of the valley, for the last mile or so.

Just beyond the church is a turning on the left which is signed simply as a dead end; what the sign neglects to tell you is that this is the turning for the hamlet of Booze. The place names along this valley are fascinating. Nearly all of them have Norse origins. Whaw, for instance, means 'the enclosure by the sheep field'. Booze, rather disappointingly, means 'the house by the bend', presumably that of the nearby beck.

The long, limestone escarpment on the far side of the river, on your left, is Fremington Edge, and just as you draw near to the foot of it you may spot a square church tower in the distance. That is Grinton again. You only get a glimpse, then the chances are you will be preoccupied for a short while as the road drops round a series of hairpin bends down a one-in-seven gradient. You cross over a narrow bridge and a mile later suddenly find yourself back in Reeth.

The road brings you in past the petrol station and – of all things, out in the heart of the Dales – a Lancia garage, and to the T-junction beside the Buck Hotel. Here we suggest you indulge yourselves and go straight across, past the wide village green. It has been a long time since passing a decent tea-shop, so why not park on the cobbled area in front of the King's Arms and explore the Copper Kettle tea-rooms?

Back on the B6270, follow the signs for *Leyburn* and *Richmond*. As you leave Reeth, you may spot a turning for Marrick, Marske and Hurst. This is an alternative route along the old road to Richmond, but as it is steep and narrow, without much in the way of views, it is not recommended. Continue along the B6270 to the A6108 and follow the road back to Richmond.

Richmond is a lovely market town, one of the finest in the north of England. With its winding streets and wide open market square, it looks rather like a continental town – French perhaps, or Spanish – and it's well worth allowing yourself a good couple of hours to explore the town and its attractions.

The castle is particularly fascinating – it's one of the oldest stone castles in the country and shouldn't be missed if you are passing through the area. There is an excellent view from the 100ft high keep, and you can see why the Normans felt this was such an excellent strategic stronghold. When they built the Great Tower, they had no scaffolding or timbers, so they built great earth ramps to haul the massive stones to the top. When the tower was completed, the ramps had to be dug away.

The town grew up around the castle, and it later gave its name to Richmond in Surrey. Incidentally, the name comes from old French, 'riche-mont' and means 'strong-hill'. The road which runs along the bottom of the market square is still called Frenchgate and is apparently where Norman civilians and traders lived after the castle was built.

Tan Hill Inn, half-way round the tour, is a complete contrast. It's the highest pub in England, 1,732ft up on the moors. It's been run for the past eight years by Margaret and Alec Baines, who try to keep it open all year round. It's not easy in winter when it can get completely cut off by snow. If you're up this way in May, it's worth calling in on the last Thursday of the month when the pub is the setting for the Tan Hill Show, the famous Swaledale sheep sales.

Tan Hill Inn, England's highest pub.

TOUR ELEVEN
~
Malham and Littondale

Malham Cove is one of the scenic

wonders of the Yorkshire Dales, a

spectacular natural amphitheatre with

240ft high limestone walls. It is one of the

most popular attractions in the National

Park. It forms a focal point for this route,

a very scenic drive which also takes in one

of Yorkshire's most distinctive mountains

and one of its loveliest dales.

Settle to Halton Gill, taking in Fountains Fell and
Pen-y-ghent, then via Littondale and Arncliffe to
Malham Tarn and Malham.
Distance: 35 miles. Driving time: 2½–3 hours

*A magnificent example of a limestone
dry valley near Malham.*

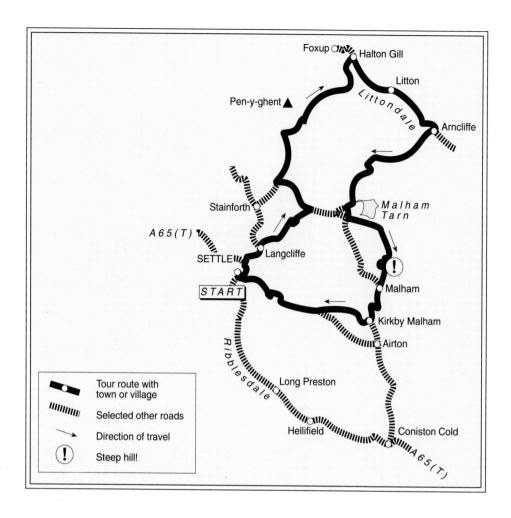

Legend:
- Tour route with town or village
- Selected other roads
- Direction of travel
- (!) Steep hill!

Map labels: Foxup, Halton Gill, Litton, Pen-y-ghent ▲, Littondale, Arncliffe, Stainforth, Malham Tarn, A65(T), SETTLE, Langcliffe, START, Malham, Kirkby Malham, Airton, Ribblesdale, Long Preston, Hellifield, Coniston Cold, A65(T)

SETTLE TO FOUNTAINS FELL

Settle is a small market town which is always bustling in the holiday season, despite being by-passed by the A65 trunk road from Kendal to Leeds. It was granted its market charter in 1248 and has a market cross in the centre of the busy main street. Just south of the cross is the Shambles, an arched, eighteenth-century building which houses the tourist information centre.

The tour starts from the market cross. Following signs for *Kendal*, head north, past the church and under the railway bridge. Look out for a sign for *Horton-in-Ribblesdale*, *Langcliffe* and *Stainforth* and turn right. This brings you into Lang-cliffe, a pretty little village with a neat village green and a well-tended Victorian church. At one time it had an inn called the Naked Woman, now long gone (although there is still a Ye Olde Naked Man café in Settle, opposite the market

cross). As you leave the centre of the village, the road becomes single track and starts its ascent in an exciting series of bends.

As you climb you get a good view into Ribblesdale on your left, with a hint of Pen-y-ghent ahead. The road levels off and meanders across very impressive limestone country. The distinctive flat top of Ingleborough comes into view and, in the far distance, you can just about spot Black Combe, on the Furness peninsula. Shortly after a cattle grid, the road goes through a narrow limestone gully and you emerge to the wonderful sight of Fountains Fell dead ahead and – to the left of Fountains – the long ridge of Pen-y-ghent.

Half a mile farther on, take care as the road descends to Cowside Farm; this can be a dangerous spot in wet or icy conditions. The road climbs again, past a rather haggard snow fence (partly

demolished by cows using it as a scratching post), and after another mile you come to a junction.

FOUNTAINS FELL AND PEN-Y-GHENT

Turn left (*Stainforth*) on to a single-track road, with Ingleborough directly ahead as you make the turn. That insignificant-looking low ridge on your left has the delightful name of Tinkling Stone Dyke; it doesn't even rate a mention on the Ordnance Survey maps.

The road drops again, working around the south-western contours of Fountains Fell. After a mile and a half, the road descends a one-in-five hill via a series of short bends and you clatter over a cattle grid before climbing to a T-junction, beside Sannat Hall Farm.

Go right (*Halton Gill*) and as you follow this road along the valley, you get an excellent view of Pen-y-ghent. Two miles from the junction, you come to a wide, grassy area where you can park, although in summer there is usually a notice up demanding a small fee. Once beyond this point there are National Park signs firmly exhorting you not to park on the grass verges.

No one seems to know the origin of Pen-y-ghent's attractive name, although the first part, Pen- (or *penno*), is Celtic for hill, leading some to claim it means 'hill of the border'. It is 2,273ft high, and one of the famous 'Three Peaks', the others being Ingleborough and Whernside. It is a fascinating mountain. A long, central ridge of hard, millstone grit has been exposed where the softer, surrounding Yoredale rock has been weathered away, giving the mountain its characteristic stepped shape. Our photographer claims it reminds him of the inverted keel of a Viking long ship, but this could be due to fumes from photographic chemicals.

PEN-Y-GHENT TO HALTON GILL

As you climb the narrow, V-shaped valley you start to see a ridge ahead of you; this is Horse Head Moor, on the far side of Littondale.

Once past Pen-y-ghent House, there

Above: The approach to Pen-y-ghent, along the Pennine Way across Fawsett Moor. Right: The pattern of fields around the River Skirfare at the head of Littondale.

is a long limestone band on your right, with Pen-y-ghent Gill running below. As you drop downhill, don't be tempted to go too fast; the road undulates and there are plenty of exciting scrape marks on the tarmac.

Two miles beyond Pen-y-ghent House, you will come to a small quarry car-park where you can stop and enjoy the view of the valley below. At the head of the valley, tucked into a sharp fold in Horse Head Moor, is Halton Gill, a small cluster of grey houses. As you follow the stream up the fell from the village, the peak looming above is Horse Head. The village stands at the foot of a pack-horse route which crosses the fell to Raisgill in Langstrothdale.

Look right and you get a lovely view along Littondale; all green fields and white limestone walls, interspersed with trees and grey field barns. These two-storey barns are a distinctive feature of the Dales, usually providing winter accommodation for stock and storage space above for feed.

You cross the River Skirfare and come to a T-junction at Halton Gill. Go right (*Litton* and *Arncliffe*) and over a narrow, humpbacked bridge. As you go down the valley, the road gets progressively narrower – if you meet any traffic you may be forced to retreat into a gateway.

LITTONDALE

This is a very green and picturesque valley. Unlike most of the other dales, there was no lead mining here. In Norman times this whole area was hunting forest, and during the medieval period it was a sheep-rearing estate for Fountains

Abbey, near Ripon (which also gave its name to Fountains Fell). The old name for the valley, used by Wordsworth, was Amerdale. In *The Water Babies*, Charles Kingsley referred to it as Vendale. More recently it featured in Yorkshire Television's rural soap opera as Emmerdale.

Once past the village of Litton, the valley opens out and you get a good view across the fields to Yew Cogar Scar (ahead and to the right). You may spot one or two cars trundling along below the escarpment – on the road you will shortly be taking.

Two miles after Litton, you come into Arncliffe. The road bears round to the right, past the turning for Hawswick – following the sign for *Kilnsey* and *Grass-ington* – and crosses a double-arched bridge over the River Skirfare.

Look out for the lovely old church, on your left, spectacularly offset by the limestone scar running across the fell

behind. It is named after St Oswald, the king of Northumbria. Born in AD 602, he established Christianity in his kingdom and assisted St Aiden in founding the monastery on Lindisfarne. Oswald was killed in the battle of Maserfield, Shropshire, in AD 642, by Penda, the pagan king of Mercia. However, his fame was such that there are churches dedicated to him all over England.

The village green is overlooked by a number of attractive houses, most of which are Grade II listed buildings. The Falcon Inn is currently trying to disguise itself under a mass of ivy, possibly to deter autograph hunters who may have spotted it in *Emmerdale Farm*.

ARNCLIFFE TO MALHAM TARN

As you reach the village green, take the turning on the right for *Malham*. As you climb the one-in-six hill it is difficult to

keep your eyes off Yew Cogar Scar on the far side of the river. Look out for what must be one of the most spectacular drystone walls in the Dales, apparently defying gravity to scale the fell. Cowside Beck runs below the escarpment, but to get a decent look at it you have to park and walk a hundred yards or so across the field. It is worth it for the dramatic view into the steep river valley.

The road traverses Nab End, the southern flank of Darnbrook Fell, and after a mile of steady climbing, you arrive at the top, from where there's a good view into the river gorge. Look at Cowside, the crag above the river, and you may spot some sheep whose greed has overcome their survival instincts. Or do all sheep have nerves of steel?

You begin a deceptively gentle descent – suddenly it becomes a one-in-five plummet, with hairpin bends. This must be tremendously exciting in winter. You

come down to Darnbrook House, and cross a bridge before arriving at the farm gate. Remember to shut it after you have gone through and don't panic if you draw the attention of a couple of highly vocal sheepdogs – they are usually chained up.

Go through the farm and follow the road as it climbs around Far Fell. By the time you have encountered another couple of gates, you are approaching Malham Moor.

MALHAM TARN AND MALHAM

This is a beautiful open moor with one or two enclosed fields, mostly belonging to the National Trust. As you approach a small wood you may catch a glimpse of Malham Tarn. Ignore the first turning to the tarn, by Water Houses, and continue around the wood.

Malham Tarn, together with over 3,000 acres of surrounding land, is owned by the National Trust. The tarn

itself, together with Tarn House, was donated to the Trust in 1946, and since 1947 they have both been let to the Field Studies Council. The main part of the house was built in the eighteenth century as a shooting lodge and it has had a number of famous visitors in its time, most notably Charles Kingsley, who used the surrounding countryside as the setting for *The Water Babies*.

Just past the wood, follow the left fork for *Malham*. As you drive along this narrow lane you lose sight of the tarn, which is just below the curiously pudding-shaped Great Close Scar, away to the left. After half a mile you come to a crossroads. The road for Malham, and Malham Cove, is straight on. This route gives lazy drivers a good view of the Cove, but we think the more interesting route is to the left, signed *Grassington*. Ignore the notice stating that the road is 'unsuitable for motor vehicles after 1.5 miles'. This refers to Mastiles Lane, as you will shortly discover.

A mile along the road there is a car-park and a footpath to Malham Tarn. This area is known as Water Sinks; the water flows from the tarn via the small beck just before the car-park, trickles across the moor and then abruptly vanishes, somewhere away to your right. The tarn itself is at most fourteen ft deep and has a low dam, built in 1791.

Just past the car-park, the road cuts across the Pennine Way, a sporadic companion on several of our tours. It was inaugurated on Malham Moor, on 24 April 1965, the culmination of a campaign which was begun in 1935 by Tom Stephenson, then countryside correspondent on the *Daily Herald* and later secretary of the Ramblers' Association from 1948 to 1968. This long-distance route was formed by the forerunner of the Countryside Commission and is over 265 miles long, starting at Edale, in Derbyshire, and ending at Kirk Yetholm, Scotland. The Scottish sec-

tion was not officially designated until 1977.

Half a mile past the car-park, the road takes a sharp right. The route to Grassington goes straight on, through the gateway and down Mastiles Lane. This was an important highway from the twelfth century onwards, originally used by the monks of Fountains Abbey to reach their holdings on Malham Moor. It continued in use right up until the late eighteenth century, when the canals and railways took over its role.

The road comes down off the moor, past the long, limestone escarpment of Goredale Scar, and after two miles brings you into the centre of Malham. You pass the Listers Arms on your right (built in 1723) and then go over a small bridge to a T-junction. Go left (*Settle, Skipton* and *Hellifield*), past the Buck Inn to the National Park information centre and car-park. Don't even think of trying to park by the road. Malham receives nearly a million visitors a year and it gets very congested if they all arrive at once.

A SHORT AND EXTREMELY EASY WALK TO MALHAM COVE

By now you are probably in need of a tea, and if you are thinking of walking through the village, it is hardly any extra effort to go and look at Malham Cove. Follow the main street, past the bridge and out of the village. After ten minutes' slog up the hill, look out for a footpath sign for the Pennine Way. Go through the gate and the path leads you to Malham Cove. Okay, so it is actually about a mile from the car-park – but wasn't it worth it? You could recover with a tea at the Malham Cove Centre, on the way back.

MALHAM TO SETTLE

Thoroughly refreshed, get back in the car and continue out of the village. Within moments you are back in an open, rural landscape.

A mile down the road you come into Kirkby Malham. As you go through the village, the road goes straight on to Settle, but it is worth taking a slight detour to the left to look at the church, from which the village takes its name – meaning literally 'the church place in Malhamdale'. The church of St Michael the Archangel seems rather grand for the village and in fact it is known as the Cathedral of the Dales. Mostly fifteenth-century, it has a pair of stone stocks in the churchyard and some entertaining Celtic heads carved above the porch.

As you leave Kirkby Malham look right and you should spot Malham Cove. The road climbs steadily for almost two miles, then you cross a cattle grid and are out on Scosthrop Moor. When you reach the second cattle grid, three-quarters of a mile later, you are at High Side, 1,260ft above sea level. Pause here for one of the most remarkable views in the north of England . . .

The long, low hill to your left is Pendle. Follow the ridge to the right and, if your eyesight is good and there is not the slightest hint of haze, you might just spot the television transmitter mast at Winter Hill, above Manchester, approximately 35 miles away. Ahead you can see Black Combe, on the other side of Barrow in Furness; a 180-degree panorama encompassing over 70 miles.

You may just be able to make out Crinkle Crags and Bowfell among the Lakeland Fells. In the more immediate foreground is Attermire Scar, just below Langcliffe Scar. That curious object in the trees, just below, is the green copper dome on the chapel of Giggleswick School.

Set off again, down to a small wood, where there is a footpath to Scaleber Force. Less than a mile beyond that, the road suddenly drops down a one-in-five incline and you get a glimpse of Settle ahead. The bends get more exciting and the road narrows as you approach the foot of the hill, after which you arrive on the outskirts of Settle. Follow the road down Victoria Street, turn left at the junction into a cobbled street, then right again and you are back at Market Place.

The drive up from Settle is very pretty and some of the roads on this tour give drivers plenty to get their teeth into. The road to Darnbrook is particularly exciting and needs to be taken with great care, especially in wet or icy conditions.

Malham Tarn is Yorkshire's second largest lake, after Hornsea Mere. It's a very quiet, peaceful spot, ideal for an afternoon's drive and a short walk. It comes as quite a shock when you drive down into Malham village and suddenly find yourself in one of the most popular Dales villages. The trick is to try and avoid it around mid-afternoon when all the coach parties seem to get there. If necessary, come back in the evening to wander around and have the place to yourself. There are a couple of excellent pubs for bar meals, and you may be interested to know that the Youth Hostel was designed by John Dower, who produced the draft plans for the creation of the British national parks.

Malham Cove is very impressive. It is a magnificent natural amphitheatre and it is well worth taking time out to explore, even if it means you have to leave the car in the village and take to travelling by foot. Make sure you pack a camera.

The drive back to Settle, from Kirkby Malham, has one of the most striking panoramas in the book; a 70-mile vista from the Lakes in the north, down into the heart of Lancashire. It is stunning, so make sure you do this tour in good weather or the last part of the drive will lose its dramatic appeal.

Malham village.

TOUR TWELVE
~
The Western Dales

This is a good, half-day tour around the western Dales, from the majestic, natural grandeur of Whernside and Ingleborough, Yorkshire's highest mountains, to the man-made splendour of the famous viaduct which carries the Settle to Carlisle railway line across Ribblehead. And if you get bored with the view above ground, there is the opportunity to go below it, in one of the show caves at Ingleton.

Sedbergh to Ribblehead, via Garsdale Head and Cowgill, then down to Chapel-le-Dale and Ingleton and back via Dent.
Distance: 45 miles. Driving Time: 3½ hours

Dentdale looking west from Monkeybeck Scar,
under Great Knoutberry Hill.

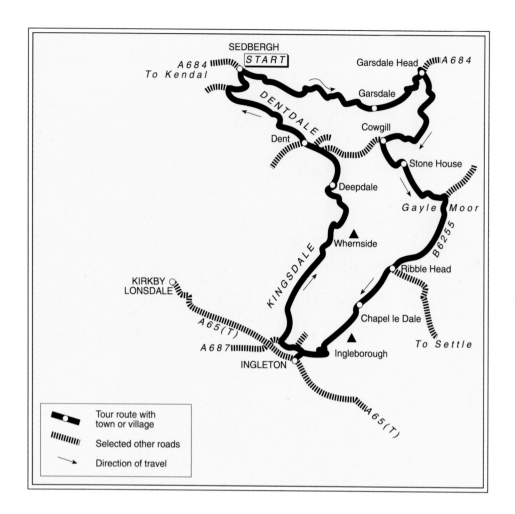

Sedbergh is an ancient town, with a system of narrow
yards, just off the main street, which date from
Tudor times. The snow-covered mountain in the
distance is Whernside.

SEDBERGH TO GARSDALE HEAD

Sedbergh is an odd little place, attractive
in its way but slightly displaced, not quite
either Lakes or Dales in character. Its
main claim to fame is the public school
which gives it the air of a college town.
Founded as a chantry school in 1525, it
became a grammar school 27 years later.
From the start, it had close links with St
John's College, Cambridge, which ap-
pointed the schoolmasters. It was rebuilt
in 1716 and became a public school in
1874. Wordsworth's son, John, attended
as a pupil, and Hartley Coleridge, son of
Samuel Taylor Coleridge, was a master
here (until he was sacked for drunken-
ness). The 1716 school house is now
Sedbergh library.

Sedbergh is situated at an important
crossroads of routes from Kendal to York
and Lancaster to Newcastle. Castlehaw,
on the north-east edge of the town, stands
on the site of a Norman castle.

The starting-point for the tour is the
Yorkshire Dales National Park information centre, in Sedbergh. Rattle across
the cobbles, down the main street to
join the A683, and go left, on to the
dual carriageway (*Kirkby Stephen* and
Hawes).

After a quarter of a mile, take the
turning on the right (*Hawes, Northallerton, Leeming Bar* and *Garsdale*), on
to the A684. This drops downhill and you
are immediately on a much narrower
road which crosses the River Rawthey
via a narrow bridge and heads off into
open countryside. There is not much in
the way of views at the start, because at
this point the road is running along the
bottom of a valley.

The road climbs gradually and after a
mile and a half you go over a cattle grid
and then are out on open moor. This
means that you are fair game for the local
sheep population, so watch out for them

getting their species muddled and play-
ing chicken in the middle of the road.
Ahead and to the left you can see the
flanks of Baugh Fell; if you follow this
back you can see the convoluted folds
of Brant Fell. Both these names are Old
English or Anglo-Saxon in origin; Baugh
Fell means 'the rounded hill', Brant Fell
means simply 'the steep mountain'.

Within half a mile you come to a large
lay-by on your left. It is well worth
parking and taking a longer look at the
view – there is usually a viewfinder which
gives the names of the surrounding
peaks (I say usually because during the
summer of 1992, when this tour was
being researched, the viewfinder was
missing – temporarily, I hope).

Clough Beck lies at the bottom of
the sharp valley, on the far side of the
lay-by from the road. From this point
you get a good view of Brant Fell and
Sedbergh and can see back to the
Lakeland fells.

Shortly afterwards the road crosses
another cattle grid and you come down
off the moor. The road is narrower here
and meanders up and down, the views
restricted to Baugh Fell on your left. As
so often in the Yorkshire Dales, you get
the impression that whoever planned the
road could not possibly have conceived
of the idea that anyone might want to get
anywhere in a hurry. There is a sharp
right-hand turn and then the road crosses
the Clough and you are into Garsdale.
There are some wonderful old barns
along here, with gaps in the walls for
ventilation. Garsdale is a small hamlet
but does boast a garage and petrol
station. Just opposite, on the other side
of the river, is the picturesque post office
and village store.

The River Clough is a bit brown and
sluggish but there is a small cascade as
you come out of the village. The hill on
the right is Snaizwold Fell; just to the left
of the conifer plantation, the Settle to
Carlisle line vanishes under the fell, into
a tunnel over half a mile long.

106

Just in case you were thinking this bit was easy, there is an avalanche warning sign a quarter of a mile beyond Garsdale. Resist the temptation to hurry past too quickly. The road runs alongside the river, and after a couple of miles crosses it and then begins to climb. As you go over the second bridge (three miles from Garsdale village) there is a turning for *Garsdale Station*. Turn right here, over a little beck, and the road starts climbing steeply, past the railway cottages and station. Just past the station, you go under the Settle–Carlisle line and the gradient gets even more exciting, the road becoming single track with passing places, to add to the fun.

GARSDALE HEAD TO COWGILL

After half a mile, the view starts to open out. As long as you don't leave the car, you can pull in by a farm gate and look back to Mallerstang and Abbotside Common. You pass the intriguingly-named Shaking Moss on your left, and, after a mile and a half of continuous climbing you reach the summit stone (there is a lay-by alongside). You have attained a height of 1,750ft.

It is all downhill from here, though it is not noticeable to begin with. Ahead you can see the Lakeland fells, looking right along Garsdale to Scafell, Bowfell, Great Gable and the Coniston range. After a while, Whernside hoves into view and you begin a more obvious descent. On a good, clear day the views are excellent, but this could be a very bleak and misty place in bad weather.

Just past the track to Monkeybeck Grains, you have Great Knoutbury Hill on your left, Rise Hill on the right and Barbon High Fell directly ahead, flanked by Whernside (on the left) and Middleton Fell. As you come off the hill, Ingleborough is on your left and you can see Cowgill below, at the head of Dentdale. As you pass the small conifer wood at Dodderham Moss, you can see a snow fence built with railway sleepers on the fell side to your right.

The road crosses over the Settle–Carlisle line and you pass Dent Station and the Station House (now privately owned – a fine example of premature privatization, when British Rail thought they were going to be allowed to let the Settle–Carlisle line fall into disuse). At 1,100ft above sea level it is the highest main line station in England.

Find low gear as the road drops down a 17% gradient. As you descend there is an excellent view of the valley, the switch-backs giving everyone in the car a good opportunity to look. There is no immediate sign of Cowgill village, but look for the church in the trees. If you stop here for a moment, look left to Attengill and Dent Head viaducts. Dent Head is just before the famous Blea Moor Tunnel.

Don't get over-confident; the road gets even steeper as you approach the valley floor. Finally you come in amongst the houses of Cowgill and arrive at a T-junction. Turning left, you go over a bridge across the River Dee and past a funny little bridge to Harbourgill Farm.

COWGILL TO RIBBLEHEAD

After passing the Sportsman's Inn you find yourself driving along the valley bottom, so for a while views are fairly limited. It is a gentle, flat road for the first half-mile or so, but gets very narrow as it crosses the Dee, just below Artengill Beck. Once over the bridge, the road goes right. A mile later, you start to climb towards Dent Head.

The viaduct seems to leap out from nowhere and soar skywards in a highly unexpected fashion. The road goes underneath and on the far side there is a tremendous view back to the viaduct and its ten arches, with Widdale Fell and Great Knoutbury in the background. If you encounter a cluster of train enthusiasts parked along here, armed with cameras and timetables, there is a fair chance that they have rung Carlisle

railway station and discovered that a steam train is due. If you are lucky enough to spot one (a steam train, that is, not an enthusiast) it is an enchanting sight.

As you climb to the top of Gayle Moor, you enter North Yorkshire, and straight ahead of you is Pen-y-ghent. You come to a T-junction with the B6255. Go right and you have the conspicuously flat summit of Ingleborough directly ahead. There is evidence of a huge Iron Age fort on the 2,372ft high plateau of Ingleborough.

The posts on either side of the road, by the way, are snow poles. They help you stay on the road in winter.

This is a gentle descent along a wide, winding road. If you have come prepared for a picnic, you could park on the grass verge, though there is a lay-by after a mile or so.

After three miles you pass Far Gearstones Farm and suddenly you are confronted with Batty Moss Viaduct – better known as Ribblehead. The road heads directly towards it and as you approach there is a lay-by on your left, just before a bridge and a turning to Horton-in-Ribblesdale and Settle. You may also find

Opposite: Dent Head viaduct, 100ft high in places, it stands over a limestone quarry, stones from which were used to build Arten Gill viaduct. Below: St Leonard's Church, Chapel-le-Dale.

an ice-cream van in summer. Continue past the lay-by and turning and you come to a car-park on your right. There is actually a track out of the back of the car-park which takes you straight to the viaduct, but it is very rough and not a public highway, so it is not recommended for cars. Park here and walk to the viaduct.

Ribblehead was built in the early 1870s to carry the line over the River Ribble. It is a quarter of a mile long and has 24 arches, the highest being 165ft above ground. The viaduct was restored in 1988–91. A plaque, unveiled on 15 June 1992, stands next to pillar 13, commemorating the achievement of the men who built the line. It was the last major railway to be built entirely by manual labour. Five thousand workers were employed, from all over the country, and they lived in shanty towns along the length of the line. They gave their temporary homes exotic names such as Salt Lake, Sebastapol, Belgravia, Jericho and Jerusalem. Over a hundred men died during the building of the line, and some of their names are recorded in the churches at Settle and Chapel-le-Dale.

RIBBLEHEAD TO INGLETON

Take care coming out of the car-park – it is an awkward turning. Continue along the B6255, past the Station Inn and under the viaduct. As you come out the other side there is another brilliant view and you can see that the viaduct actually curves. On the back of Whernside, to your right, you can see a massive, eroded path, the legacy of the Three Peaks Race and innumerable fell walkers.

The route runs straight for a while, following the course of a Roman road. There is an impressive limestone escarpment on your left. After a mile and a half, the road drops downhill, past the Old House Inn, and then you come level with a small wood. Look out for the turning on the right for *Chapel-le-Dale church*. Turn

A frozen waterfall in Deepdale Beck. Deepdale is a narrow valley, squeezed between Whernside and Great Coum, which once supported a thriving woollens industry.

right here, into a very narrow lane, and you will come to the very pretty church of St Leonard's.

The church is around 400 years old and is almost invisible from the road, hidden by trees. This is an attractive spot, full of atmosphere.

From the church, continue along the narrow lane, past the farms and over a cattle grid. There is a sign on the wall stating that the cattle grid is private property and that you use it at your own risk; but there can't be that many motorists who take the trouble to open the gate alongside.

As you drive along the lane, with Ingleborough on your left, you are following part of the old turnpike road from Richmond to Lancaster. Nowadays the main route along the valley is the B6255. The views along this part of the route are very pleasant, but ultimately frustrating because you can't stop and get out; there are dire warnings against parking on the grass verge. After a mile and a half you pass a tiny car-park for the limestone scar on your right, but somehow it is not very inviting.

While driving along, you may spot a building on the far side of the valley, below Ingleborough, with the word CAVES painted on its roof. This stands by the entrance to White Scar Cave, one of the area's best-known show caves, discovered in 1923. It contains one stalagmite reputed to be over 225,000 years old. (To get to White Scar, continue straight on at Chapel-le-Dale, instead of turning off at St Leonard's church.)

Approaching Ingleton, you come level with some quarry workings, but the wall on your left mercifully obscures the site. Shortly afterwards, you pass footpath signs to Thornton Force and Beezley Falls. If you fancy a walk, Beezley Falls is the closer of the two.

The road drops down a one-in-eight incline, through a wood, and brings you to the outskirts of Ingleton. At the T-junction on Mill Lane, go right and you come to the car-park for the Waterfalls Walk.

INGLETON TO DENT

You have to pay to do the Waterfalls Walk, irrespective of whether you park your car here or not. However, further round this tour there is a way to do the walk for free. The walk is a legacy of the Ingleborough Improvement Society, who in the 1880s went round building footbridges and generally tidying up the landscape to make it attractive to Victorian tourists.

Continue past the car-park, under the viaduct and out of Ingleton. After half a mile, you come to a turning on the right for *Thornton-in-Lonsdale* and *Dent*. Turn right here on to an even narrower minor road, overgrown and grassy in places. You go past a funny little church with a tower topped by a spire. This is St Oswald's. Turn right (*Dent*) just past the church and as you make the turning look out for the old stocks in the grass verge, by the churchyard wall.

The road climbs gently and Ingleborough comes back into view. Unfortunately, the higher you climb the better the view of the quarries above Ingleton. After a mile and a half you start to descend again. Look out for a grassy track on your right and a public footpath sign for *Thornton Force*. There is room for two or three cars to park off the road here, and if you follow the track and the footpath, you come to the top of the Waterfalls Walk signed in Ingleton. It is a lovely walk, so allow half an hour and follow the signs for Thornton Force. They lead you off the track and across the fields to a spectacular little waterfall. If you're lucky, just before you leave the track you may encounter an ice-cream van, apparently parked in the middle of nowhere (but in reality this entrepreneur is displaying immense commercial acumen).

The minor road continues uphill. You are now travelling up Kingsdale and in front is Whernside, Yorkshire's highest mountain (2,416ft). If it is a bright,

sunny day you may need sunglasses just to look at all the white drystone walls.

As you approach Kingsdale Head Farm, over four miles into the valley, you suddenly realize that we have omitted to tell you something vital: this is a gated road. There are four gates in all. Make sure you close them all after you, and think of it as good exercise.

After the first gate, past the farm, the countryside gets rougher, more hilly. The road undulates alarmingly for a mile, and then you go steeply uphill to gate number two. This has a sign on it which reads: 'If you've time to come this way, you've time to shut the gate.' (To which some wag has added: 'If of this problem you want to be rid, why not install a cattle grid?')

A mile farther on you come to the top of Kingsdale. Two more ridges lie ahead of you, and on the other side of them is Dentdale. Ahead you can see Rise Hill, East Baugh Fell and, to the right of that, Abbotside Common.

The road starts to drop quite steeply. There is a lovely view of Deepdale below you with its superb patterns of fields, the walls running across the landscape as if drawn with a ruler. Three-quarters of a mile into the descent you come to the third gate. Only one more to go. The next bit of road gets very exciting as it plummets towards Gatesgarth Beck Bottom. You drop down to the beck and have a chance to get your breath back while someone opens gate number four.

Continue through the farm and you come into a really pretty valley. Make the best of the views because you lose them after a mile or so. The road brings you to a T-junction. Go left (*Dent*) and after another three-quarters of a mile you will come into the village of Dent.

DENT TO SEDBERGH

The road takes you into the centre of the village, where you come to a cobbled street. This leads you round to the right, past the post office and the George and Dragon Hotel. You will pass a large block of pink Shap granite and a drinking fountain in the wall on your right – a memorial to Adam Sedgwick. He was born in Dent in 1785 and was Woodwardian Professor of Geology at Cambridge for 55 years, until his death in 1873.

Turn left by the memorial, keeping to the cobbled street, and after passing the Sun Inn you return to a tarmac road surface. Look out for the National Park car-park on your right if you feel like doing some exploring on foot.

Dent is one of those pretty little villages where it is easy to imagine that you have seen it all as you drive through. Wrong. There are all sorts of little shops tucked away off the main street, but it is still hard to imagine that Dent – or Dent Town, as it is sometimes known – was once more important than Sedbergh. Stone Close Tea Shop is a good place to start exploring. It is a fascinating seventeenth-century building and apart from anything else is the home of wonderful home-baked scones . . .

Tea stop over, continue out of Dent. Rise Hill, on your right, is very impressive seen from this angle. As you drive out, you are looking along a long, flat valley ahead. The road crosses over the River Dee (which seems like an old friend by now) and the views open out, with Middleton Fell on the left and the distinctive shape of Holme Knott ahead.

You pass Dent Craft Centre, situated in a large converted barn, and after another three miles start to approach Sedbergh. Once over the River Rawthey, carry on into the town until you come to a T-junction, just opposite the Post Horn Tea Room. Turn right and you are back on the cobbled main street of Sedbergh.

It is difficult to avoid the temptation of at least one walk on this tour. Take a picnic, make a day of it and finish up with tea at Stone Close, in Dent. You should also make sure you have at least one fit and willing passenger on board to open the gates on the stretch up Kingsdale, between Ingleton and Dent.

The high spot of the tour is undoubtedly the magnificent sight of the Ribblehead viaduct. I was brought up in the era of the steam train and although I'm not one for train-spotting, I use trains a lot now and can see the romance in steam transport. The Settle to Carlisle line is probably the most scenic railway route in the country and well worth taking if you fancy some time off from driving. It has a fascinating history. It was built between 1869 and 1875 by the Midland Railway Company, who wanted to compete with the Great Northern Railway's east coast route and the west coast line run by the North Western Railway. The aim was to build a line from London to Scotland via Bedford and Derby. The Settle to Carlisle section was a tremendous undertaking: 72 miles, twelve tunnels and fifteen viaducts. Six of the viaducts are 200yds long (Ribblehead is even longer at 440yds). Blea Moor Tunnel is 2,629yds long and 500ft deep at its deepest point. The line's highest point is 1,169ft at Garsdale Head. The cost of the line was £3,500,000; an absolute fortune for the period. Beeching's axe fell in 1963 and by 1970 only Settle and Appleby stations stayed open to through trains. In recent years, immense public pressure has persuaded British Rail and the government to reconsider selling it off and it now operates as a highly successful tourist attraction in its own right.

Dent village.

113

TOUR THIRTEEN
~
Wharfedale, Middleham and Nidderdale

This is a tour of the fascinating countryside on the eastern edge of the Yorkshire Dales, from Grassington, in the heart of Wharfedale, to Middleham and Nidderdale, which lie outside the National Park boundary. It is an area rich in historical associations; Richard III lived at Middleham Castle and, centuries before, Cistercian monks founded an abbey at Jervaulx, near East Witton.

Grassington to Middleham, via Kettlewell and Coverdale – then around to Jervaulx Abbey and Masham and back along Nidderdale to Pateley Bridge and Grassington.
Distance: 61 miles. Driving time: 3½ hours

Gouthwaite Reservoir and nature reserve, Nidderdale, south of Lofthouse.

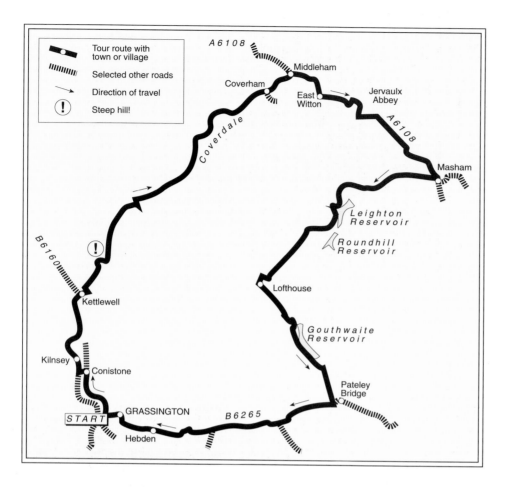

Map legend:
- Tour route with town or village
- Selected other roads
- Direction of travel
- (!) Steep hill!

A6108
Middleham
Coverham
East Witton
Jervaulx Abbey
A6108
Masham
Coverdale
Leighton Reservoir
Roundhill Reservoir
B6160
(!)
Kettlewell
Lofthouse
Kilnsey
Gouthwaite Reservoir
Conistone
START
GRASSINGTON
B6265
Pateley Bridge
Hebden

GRASSINGTON

If you approach Grassington from Skipton and cross the River Wharfe via Grassington Bridge, the main road skirts past the centre and you miss the best part of town. This doesn't stop the road getting cluttered with parked cars, so drive on to the National Park car-park, a little farther along the Pateley Bridge road. Grassington is a popular little town lying at the heart of Wharfedale, and its cobbled square and picturesque alleys are an irresistible draw in summer. The best time to visit is early morning or late evening, when the coaches have gone home.

Grassington began in the twelfth century as a collection of farms and boomed during the lead mining years of the eighteenth and nineteenth centuries. In 1902 it was linked to Skipton by the Yorkshire Dales Railway, but the line closed 28 years later.

The town gained a market charter as early as 1282 and regular markets were held until 1860. The square was the original market-place and is now a conservation area and home of the Wharfedale Folk Museum. There is actually a stream running under the cobbles, and although the water pump is now only for decoration it was operational until the 1930s. Just below the Devonshire Hotel is Grassington Old Hall. Built by Robert de Plumpton as a hunting-lodge in the thirteenth century, this is one of the oldest inhabited houses in the Dales.

If you are hunting for the Anglican church, you won't find it in the town; St Michael's and All Angels stands half a mile from the centre, on the southern bank of the River Wharfe, and is shared with the nearby village of Linton.

GRASSINGTON TO KETTLEWELL

The tour begins from the National Park car-park. Turn left out of the car-park, along the B6265 and past the entrance to

the Square. Almost immediately afterwards, turn right for *Kettlewell* and *Conistone*. This minor road is unsuitable for goods vehicles and coaches – and I can think of no higher recommendation. There is another small car-park on the left as you make the turning.

You are out of Grassington very quickly and can look over the fields and drystone walls to the River Wharfe and the head of the valley. A mile from town you enter Grass Wood, a nature reserve run by the Yorkshire Naturalist Trust. Although there is public access via a couple of ladder stiles, there is nowhere to park.

As you drive along the narrow country lane you can see across the river to Malham Moor and the white limestone crag at Kilnsey. The Mastiles Road is up there somewhere, crossing the moor from Malham Tarn to Kilnsey, part of a monastic route which passed through Grassington to Fountains Abbey.

At Conistone bear left through the village (following the sign for *Kettlewell*), cross the bridge and at the T-junction turn right on to the B6160 (*Kettlewell* and *Aysgarth*). Kilnsey Crag is straight in front of you, actually overhanging the road, and can be very distracting in summer when it is swarming with brightly-clothed rock-climbers.

Half a mile beyond the crag, you cross the River Skirfare and are passing the entrance to Littondale. The road winds to the east of Knipe Scar and continues up Wharfedale. Look ahead and slightly right and you will see Great Whernside. As you drive up the valley, the field patterns are startlingly regular. Even on overcast days the white of the stone walls set against the deep green fields brightens up the view.

An attractive, double-arched bridge takes you over the Wharfe and into Kettlewell.

KETTLEWELL TO COVERDALE
Directly over the bridge there is a National Park car-park just behind the petrol station. Continue through the village, past the turning on the right

signed *Church*, over a humpbacked bridge and turn right by the Bluebell Hotel (*Leyburn* and *Coverdale*).

Kettlewell is an attractive village, now a National Park designated conservation area, which entitles it to special planning restrictions and conservation grants. The Over and Under Outdoor Shop is the Park's Local Information Point (a sort of part-time tourist information centre). The village stands on a crossroads of pack-horse routes and was once a thriving market town, more important than Grassington, with 13 inns.

At the crossroads go straight across (*Leyburn*) and make sure you are in low gear; the next half-mile consists of one-in-four gradients with hairpin bends. Passengers get a lovely view of Park Gill Beck and Langcliffe Scar, but the driver will be too busy to look. Take special care in autumn, when wet leaves can make the road treacherous.

A mile after the road has levelled off, you start to climb another pair of hairpin bends. This stretch is known as Park Rash and ascends Cam Head, out of the head of the valley, on to North Moor. The scar away to your right is Great Whernside, and as you approach the top there is a wonderful limestone band running along the skyline on the left; it traverses the head of the valley in front of you and is picked up by a drystone wall which marches off across Whernside. It almost looks like a tide mark.

Once over the cattle grid, you are at Tor Pike, on the top of the moor, and have entered the old county of Richmondshire. The stone pillars on either side of the road seem to be for the cows to drink from, a sort of bovine bird bath. Or perhaps someone has a better explanation . . . This is a very open, windswept plateau, desolate in winter but with an attractive range of colours in springtime. You can see the road snaking off across the moor in the distance and you may spot the old mine workings, away to your left.

Half a mile from the Richmondshire sign, you pass a tall, weathered lump of stone by the roadside, known as the Hunter's Stone. This is a medieval guide post erected on the monastic route between Kettlewell and Coverham Abbey. If you look carefully, you may find the cross carved near the top.

The road winds across the moor, Cow Side and Great Whernside looming over to the right. The plateau of Whernside looks ancient and brooding. If you have already driven the twelfth tour you may be feeling puzzled; there is another Whernside – one of the famous Three Peaks – in the south-east corner of the Dales, above Ingleton. Great Whernside is its lesser cousin: 2,306ft compared to Whernside's loftier 2,416. Just to add to the family, you can see a smaller peak, ahead and to the right, called Little Whernside.

Two miles from the Hunter's Stone,

you go over a little humpbacked bridge and there is a track to Coverhead Farm on your left. This used to be known as Hunter's Hall, and the story went that every time its clock struck twelve, the Hunter's Stone turned round.

Once over the bridge, there is a short, unexpected climb and then you begin the descent into Coverdale.

COVERDALE TO MIDDLEHAM

There are a number of small hamlets dotted along the valley, many of them little more than farms and isolated clusters of cottages. The first is Wood-ale, by which time the little beck which had followed you down from the moor has become the wide, meandering River Cover.

The first substantial village you come to is Horsehouse – well, it has a pub and a post office – which was once a staging post on the pack-horse route from Wharfedale to Middleham. It is hard to believe that in the seventeenth century the valley was part of the major route between Richmond and London. Traffic has declined somewhat in the intervening 300 years.

Continuing down the valley you encounter the narrow streets of Carl-ton, the largest of Coverdale's villages. It is a pretty spot and there is a National Park car-park just beyond the Forester's Arms pub. There is a 40mph speed restriction through Carlton but this is completely unrealistic – it should be 20mph at most.

Ignore the turning on the left for Melmerby – this is not a cunning diver-sion to the tea-shop in the eighth tour – and as you leave the village the road is virtually single-track. After a couple of miles, you pass a turning on the right for Coverham and Caldbergh and the dis-used church of Holy Trinity. The road to Coverham is extremely narrow and not recommended. On the far side of the river are the ruins of Coverham Abbey,

founded in the early thirteenth century.

After another half-mile you drive past a small, reedy tarn and find yourself on Middleham Low Moor, the fifteenth-century deer park for the lords of Middleham. Less than a mile later, you can see the intriguing ruins of Middleham rising above the town.

EXPLORING MIDDLEHAM

You come into Middleham and pass an old stone cross, commemorating the granting of the market charter in 1479 by Richard, Duke of Gloucester (later Richard III). It is called the Swine's Cross and the rather eroded figure on top of the pillar is a boar, the emblem of the family of Richard's wife, Anne Neville. Continue through the town, past the fountain and the old school house – the area known as Upper Square – to a T-junction. Carry straight on and you are in Lower Square, with its second market cross and the central cobbled parking area. Abandon the car here and explore.

Middleham Castle stands above the town, backing on to green fields. From the square, an archway beside the Nosebag Tea Room leads into a narrow back alley which takes you up to the castle. Look out for the farrier, just opposite the castle entrance.

It is an impressive structure, more so in its way than the castle at Richmond, probably because it seems so out of scale with the town. The oldest part is the keep, built in 1170 by Ralph, son of the first Lord of Middleham. In 1471, the castle was granted to Richard, Duke of Gloucester, who was then only 19. He lived here between 1472 and 1482. When Edward IV died in 1483, Richard contested the crown and became King Richard III in the same year. His reign lasted just 25 months; on 22 August 1485, he met the army of Henry Tudor at Bosworth and was killed in battle. Henry Tudor was crowned King Henry VII. The castle was dismantled after the Civil War and the only inhabitants now are pigeons.

Middleham's other claim to fame is its horse-racing, which dates back to the early years of the eighteenth century. (Horse breeding in the area has an even longer history; the monks of Jervaulx kept horses in the Forest of Wensleydale in the twelfth century.) There was a race-course in use on Middleham Moor until 1873 and this was the Newmarket of its day. It is still one of the North's great training centres and you can often see racehorses training in the early morning on Middleham Low and High Moors.

MIDDLEHAM TO MASHAM

Set off down through the Lower Square, past the Black Bull Inn and out of town, following the signs for *Masham*. A mile or so later, you go over a narrow hump-backed bridge and cross the River Cover for the last time, just above the point at which it joins the River Ure.

You pass through East Witton and a mile or so later start to pick up signs for Jervaulx Abbey. You'll encounter Jervaulx Hall first – on your left – and then come to Abbey Hall Gardens car-park and café, a hundred yards farther on, on the right. The Abbey stands on the opposite side of the road to the car-park; cross to a small iron gate and a public footpath leads you across the park to the entrance to the Abbey grounds. The Abbey and its grounds are privately owned and there is an honesty box by the gate.

The Abbey is a melancholy place, a jumble of ruined walls and arches, overgrown with ivy and wild flowers. It dates back to 1156 and was founded by John de Kinstan, a Cistercian monk. The odd name is a Norman-French corruption of 'Yore vale'. It grew in importance and at one time owned half the valley, its influence extending far into Wensleydale. Its monks are reputed to have started the long history of cheese-making in that valley. It suffered badly during the Dissolution of the Monasteries, for Henry VIII held a particular grudge against the last Abbot, Adam Sedbar, and made sure the Abbey was thoroughly dismantled.

There are park benches along the edge of the grounds, overlooking a beautiful park, and on a sunny day it is a lovely spot for a picnic.

Continue along the A6108, a swift and entertaining road which runs through

Nidderdale lies outside the boundary of the Yorkshire Dales National Park but is protected by being designated an Area of Outstanding Natural Beauty.

pleasant, open farm land for another four and a half miles to Masham. As you enter the outskirts of town, look out for the turning to *Fearby*, *Healy* and *Leighton*. The tour goes up this lane to Nidderdale, but if you want to look at Masham, carry on past the petrol station and turn right (*Masham*). If you follow the road round and then go left, you arrive in Masham's enormous Market Place.

This owes its size to the twice yearly toll-free fair and market, granted in 1393. The lack of fee attracted custom to Masham at the expense of surrounding market towns. If you arrive here on a Wednesday, make a note of where you leave your car; when the market is in progress the square is packed with people and parked vehicles.

Masham is also famous as the home of Theakston's Brewery and Old Peculier ale, which takes its name from the Court Peculier, Masham's own ecclesiastical court which upheld religious laws in the town in medieval times.

MASHAM TO PATELEY BRIDGE

Leaving Masham square, go back the way you came (*Middleham*), turn left at the main road and left again at the turning for *Fearby*, *Healy* and *Leighton*. The first four miles are not very exciting, but once past the village of Healy the scenery improves and you find yourself heading back into the hills.

You skirt Leighton Reservoir, cross the dam and then drive past Roundhill Reservoir. Look up at the long ridge on your left and you can't fail to spot a tall, Gothic tower standing over the hill. Disappointingly, it is just a siting tower, not a historic monument. That is where the water from the reservoir is pumped down the pipeline to Harrogate.

The tower dominates the view for the next two miles as you climb up on to Pott Moor, a very open, mossy stretch of countryside. You're not up here for long before you begin the descent towards

On the drinking fountain:

IF YOU WANT TO BE
HEALTHY
WEALTHY AND
STOUT USE
PLENTY OF COLD
WATER INSIDE
AND OUT
LET ANIMAL AND
MAN DRINK FREELY

The village of Lofthouse developed as a grange for Fountains Abbey, but today most of the permanent residents are employed by Yorkshire Water Authority.

Lofthouse. When you get your first view of the valley, look to the right and you should catch a glimpse of the dam at Scarhouse Reservoir, below Great Whernside.

There are some lovely views, which doesn't help when you're negotiating hairpin bends and the front of the car seems to be pointing straight down. You come down into a grassy meadow at the bottom of the valley, with the little hamlet of Middlesmoor on the hill to your right. It has an enormous church for such an isolated place that can be reached only by a one-in-four hill.

After half a mile you come to Lofthouse and the chances are that you will find your way barred by a gate. Don't forget to close it after you. Go through the narrow street to the T-junction. *How Stean Gorge* is signed right, *Pateley Bridge* left.

Although the route south is pleasant enough, more spectacular scenery is to be found at the head of the valley, to the north. The River Nidd starts its descent from Scarhouse Reservoir three miles upstream from here, and you can follow a road right up to the dam, where there is a car-park and picnic area. The river cuts through a narrow gorge which has earned the valley the nickname 'Little Switzerland'. There is a drawback to this detour; you have to pay to use the road, which is owned by Yorkshire Water. So if you don't fancy the trek to the reservoir, go right for a few hundred yards to where you can park (for another fee, unfortunately), and take a walk to the waterfall at How Stean Gorge.

The tour continues down through Lofthouse (left at the junction, signed *Pateley Bridge*) and as you leave the village you get a glimpse of the River Nidd on your right. Its engaging name comes from the Celtic word for 'bright'.

Lofthouse suffers from the presence of the water works and a large number of houses used as holiday homes. The next village, Ramsgill, has much more of a real, Dales air about it, with an attractive village green and the ivy-covered Yorke Arms Hotel.

Just beyond Ramsgill, the road runs alongside Gouthwaite Reservoir, the first of the dale's water supply reservoirs, opened by Bradford Corporation in 1899. It is now a nature reserve and bird sanctuary, so there is no public access. Beyond Gouthwaite, the valley becomes wider and more open, and after two miles you come into Pateley Bridge.

PATELEY BRIDGE TO GRASSINGTON

At the T-junction, beside Nidderdale Motors, our route goes right (*Grassington* and *Skipton*), but if you turn left (*Ripon* and *Harrogate*) you can do a quick detour into the town centre, explore the narrow, picturesque main street and investigate the Upper Nidderdale Museum. Back at the junction, head out of town on the B6265 (*Grassington* and *Skipton*).

A mile into the long, one-in-six climb up Greenhow Hill, you get a terrific view back to Pateley Bridge and Nidderdale. You climb steadily for a total of two miles before the road levels off and you pass the village of Greenhow. This very enjoyable B road romps across Bewerley and Craven Moors and past a number of isolated farms, any of which would be a good place to live if you don't tend to get on with your neighbours.

After four and a half miles a small building hoves into view, probably surrounded by coaches. This is the entrance to Stump Cross Caverns, one of the Dales' three major show caves. It was discovered when mine workings opened into a natural cave.

The road starts to drop away, again reaching one-in-six in places, with a wide expanse of moor on either side of the road. The distinctive ridge ahead is Barden Moor, and to your right you may catch a glimpse of Grimthwaite Reservoir. The road takes you through the village of Hebden, then there is a final short climb before you enter Wharfedale and drop back into Grassington.

Grassington is a very attractive spot and worth spending some time in. It's also an excellent base for exploring the area, and if you stay overnight, you can see it at its best, when the crowds have gone. The quaint village centre is rather spoilt by traffic, so if you're here for the day, try to park elsewhere. Don't just stick to the village centre, try exploring some of the back lanes as well, particularly up the hill. There's a very useful town trail guide available from the tourist information centre.

Don't be tempted to by-pass Middleham – it's a lovely village with an intriguing castle. The castle is an impressive building, more so in its way than the castle at Richmond, probably because it seems so large in comparison with the size of the town. Once over the grassy ditch – which is all that remains of the moat – and through the gatehouse, you'll find most of the walls, or at least the foundations are present and you can get a very good idea of the layout. Take a torch and peer into some of the rooms in the curtain wall. The keep is the oldest part of the castle and was built around 1170. Climb the 86 steps to the top and there is a wonderful view over the town and the surrounding countryside. As you look south you can almost imagine the enemy lining the ridge, preparing to attack.

The Abbey at Jervaulx is another fascinating ruin, with a quiet, dignified sense of history. The overgrown vegetation seems to be the only thing keeping up some of the walls.

Real ale enthusiasts will find the Brewery Visitor Centre at Masham interesting though I'm not a beer drinker myself, despite once being married to a brewery heiress!

The drive across the moors between Pateley Bridge and Grassington can be exhilarating in the right conditions, though it can be bleak in winter. Greenhow is one of the highest villages in England, at 1,300ft above sea level.

Jervaulx Abbey.

123

TOUR FOURTEEN
~
Hawes and Wensleydale

In 1970, James Herriot published *If Only They Could Talk*, a semi-autobiographical novel describing his life and pre-war experiences as a partner in Siegfried Farnon's veterinary practice. It was the first in a series of tales which became best sellers throughout the world and have been the basis for two feature films and the BBC television series, *All Creatures Great and Small*. To many people, the countryside around Wensleydale is forever linked with James Herriot.

From Hawes to Buckden, via Langstrothdale and Hubberholme, along Bishopdale to Aysgarth and Carperby, a short detour to Bolton Castle and then back via Askrigg and Bainbridge.
Distance: 41 miles. Driving time: 2 hours

Looking down the open road before descending into Langstrothdale from Oughtershaw Side.

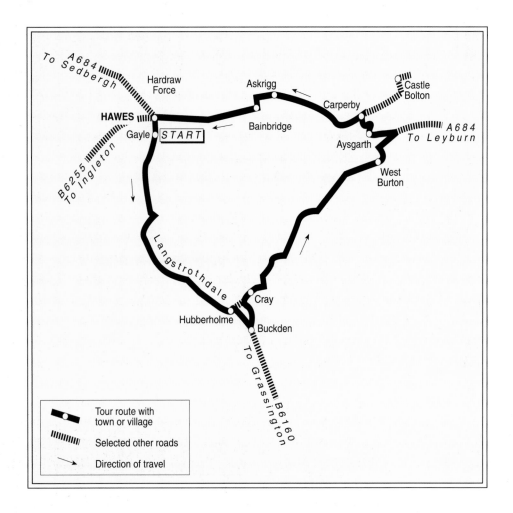

Legend:
- Tour route with town or village
- Selected other roads
- Direction of travel

Map labels: A684 To Sedbergh, Hardraw Force, Askrigg, Castle Bolton, Carperby, HAWES, Bainbridge, A684 To Leyburn, Gayle, START, Aysgarth, B6255 To Ingleton, West Burton, Langstrothdale, Cray, Hubberholme, Buckden, To Grassington B6160

HAWES

Hawes is one of the most popular villages in the Dales and can get very hectic in mid-summer. Like Ambleside, in the Lakes, it is not only a major draw in its own right but stands on a major route through the National Park. Its name comes from 'hause' or pass, dating from the days before the Lancaster to Richmond turnpike road was built and the village began to grow to the size it is today.

In 1878 it was linked by railway line to Leyburn. The line closed to passenger traffic in 1954, and finally closed down altogether ten years later, but in 1979 the engine shed was converted into the Upper Dales Folk Museum (now extended and renamed the Dales Countryside Museum). The former station building is the National Park tourist information centre. The museum and car-park are at the eastern end of the village, down the narrow lane beside W.R. Outhwaite and Son, the famous Hawes ropemakers.

The dale's major export in recent times – apart from a certain vet – is, of course, Wensleydale cheese which until recently was made in Hawes. Its association with the village goes back to 1898, but in 1992 Dairy Crest – with singular disregard for tradition and the concerns of local industry – decided to move production to Lancashire. Fortunately, after a management buy-out, the production of Wensleydale cheese continues at the original dairy.

The open-air Brass Band Contest is one of the more entertaining annual events, held in early September. First staged in 1881, it takes place in the natural amphitheatre at Hardraw Scar.

HAWES TO HUBBERHOLME

From the busy centre of Hawes, go west along the main street, as if heading towards Sedbergh. Turn left for *Gayle* and *Kettlewell*, just before the Burmah petrol station, and then drive past the car-park and up out of the village.

As you enter the small hamlet of Gayle, follow the road round to the left (*Kettlewell*) and over a bridge. There is a group of attractive houses on the right and a pretty little waterfall in Duerley Beck. James Herriot describes the village in *Let Sleeping Vets Lie*, when he and his new wife, Helen, spend the first day of their working honeymoon testing the local cattle.

The narrow lane climbs a one-in-six hill, past a group of farm buildings, and once out of the village you get a good view to the moors. After what feels like a long mile and a half, you can look across Cocklee Fell to Pen-y-ghent. As the road bears round to the left, ignore the turning to Cam Houses, the route of a Roman road which traverses Oughtershaw Side.

Half a mile beyond the turning there is a car-park with a viewpoint. Take a few deep breaths because the road soon begins a one-in-six plunge to Oughtershaw. This is not a very relaxing road in winter.

You descend through Oughtershaw and after another mile reach the valley bottom, where there is a National Trust sign proclaiming that you are now entering Upper Wharfedale. This is very pretty limestone scenery – the uniform green fields broken up by stone walls, field barns and the occasional farmhouse.

After a mile, you cross the river and enter Langstrothdale Chase. The long, low fell ahead of you is Buckden Pike, the beginning of Wharfedale. The river is still close to the road and, if you fancy a paddle, there is plenty of room to park on the grass verge. After a mile, there is a neat stone pack-horse bridge leading to Yockenthwaite House and then the road climbs for a mile. Like many of the places along here, Yockenthwaite is a Norse name,

Above: The River Wharfe starts out as a shallow beck at the head of Langstrothdale. Left: One of Thompson's mice in the church of St Michael and All Angels, Hubberholme.

meaning 'Yoghan's clearing'.

As you drop from the top of Langstrothdale, you can see the village of Hubberholme ahead – your first view is likely to be the church tower in amongst the trees.

HUBBERHOLME
TO BISHOPDALE

Entering the village, you see the George Inn straight in front of you and there is a road on the left which leads to the church and connects with the B6160. It is a very narrow, awkward road, so we recommend continuing straight on to Buckden. However, it is worth stopping to have a look at the church.

Hubberholme has a good, meaty

sound to it and, like Yockenthwaite, this is another place once settled by the Norse – the name means 'Hunberg's homestead'. The church dates from around 1550 and has some interesting features, including a rare sixteenth-century roodloft (a sort of decorated gallery) and attractive iron candelabras. You can have fun searching along the oak pews for Thompson's Mouse, the carved trademark of the famous craftsman from Kilburn. Until 1965, the church owned the George Inn, opposite, and the landlord was also the vicar.

On Christmas Day each year the local farmers bid for the tenancy of the field behind the Inn, a thousand-year-old tradition known locally as The Hubberholme Parliament.

A mile beyond the church, you cross Buckden Bridge and enter the village. At the road junction, just opposite the Buck Inn, turn left (*Aysgarth* and *Leyburn*) and

Some of the stone barns are centuries old and are
used to store hay and provide winter housing for cattle.
The barns vary in size and style throughout
the Yorkshire Dales.

just past the village stores is the National
Park car-park.

Buckden takes its name from the
extensive hunting forest established in
Langstrothdale by the Normans in the
twelfth century. The forest (or 'Chase')
extended the length of the valley and into
Wharfedale. A stone cross a mile below
Buckden marks its southern boundary.
The village was the Forest Officials'
residence and consisted of a hunting
lodge surrounded by a few foresters'
dwellings.

As you leave Buckden, Rakes Wood –
on your right – is one of the few remaining
signs of the hunting forest. Above it is the
steep, 1,500ft climb to Buckden Pike.
You are now on the B6160, and half a
mile from Buckden you meet the road
from Hubberholme. You can see the
church above the trees again on your left.

You climb up through Cray village,
which stands beneath the limestone scar
of Cow Close, and continue the steep
ascent to the summit of Kidstones Pass.
Look out for all the tiny waterfalls. If you
look back down the valley the road seems
to drop through a series of limestone
terraces. Naughtberry Hill, on your right,
is an impressive series of peaks, culminating in Buckden Pike. As you reach the
summit, Kidstones Scar is on your left
and Bishopdale Head on the right. Below
you is Bishopdale.

BISHOPDALE AND AYSGARTH

Now there is a long, steep descent, lasting
almost two miles. As the road crosses
Bishopdale Beck, you are officially in
Bishopdale. This is a wide, U-shaped
valley, patterned with fields and walls and
innumerable dales barns, and as you
drive along it you can speculate about
what it must have been like in the Middle
Ages when this too was all hunting forest.
It formed part of the Honour of Middleham up until the early seventeenth
century when it was broken up by
Charles I, who sold it to the citizens of

London. They didn't want it, so they sold it in lots to the yeoman farmers of the dale. Many of the fine farmhouses to be seen in the area date from that period.

After two and a half miles you come into the village of West Burton. The village centre is down the turning on the right. It's a one-way lane, so it makes a nice detour. The houses are grouped round a very pretty green and there is a distinctive market cross in the centre – an elongated stone cone topped by a weather vane, built in 1820.

Follow the road round the green, past the village shop, and it brings you back to the B6160. Turn right and after two hundred yards turn left on to the minor road (*Aysgarth* and *Hawes*). This goes over Bishopdale Beck to the junction with the A6804, the main road through Wensleydale. Turn left and follow the road towards Aysgarth.

Wensleydale is the only Yorkshire dale not to take its name from a beck or river – it's named after the small hamlet of Wensley, five miles east of here. This was the market town of the dale until ravaged by plague in the sixteenth century.

Entering Aysgarth, take the turning on the right for (deep breath) *Aysgarth Falls, Carperby, Bolton Castle, Redmore* and *Castle Bolton*. Go past the first car-park and the church, over the bridge and continue uphill for another 100yds to the National Park information centre and car-park. Park here and walk back to the bridge to investigate Aysgarth Falls.

Although not the largest, these water-falls are probably the most popular in the Yorkshire Dales. The River Ure descends a series of limestone terraces through a narrow, wooded gorge to form three named waterfalls. There are two footpaths leading down from the bridge, and if you only have time to walk one, the Middle and Lower Falls are the most impressive.

The building by the bridge was origin-ally a cotton mill – as you might guess from the name of the craft shop. It was built in 1784, though rebuilt and ex-tended a couple of times in the nineteenth century, and now houses a coach and carriage museum.

The Lower Falls, Aysgarth, where the River Ure cuts a broad passage through a shallow, limestone ravine to create the Yorkshire Dales's most popular waterfall.

From the car-park, continue up the darkly wooded hill towards Carperby. When you get to the T-junction you have a choice to make. You could go left, directly to Askrigg, but the turning right goes via Carperby to Castle Bolton . . . and Bolton Castle. That's intrigued you, hasn't it? It's only a six-mile detour and well worth it. Decision taken, turn right.

DETOUR TO CASTLE BOLTON

Carperby is a linear village, a long main street culminating in the village green. It was granted its market charter in 1305, but declined after Askrigg gained one in 1587. However, there must have been enough of a revival to make it worth erecting the market cross in 1674. At the far end of the green is St Matthew's Well, dated 1867, and as you leave the village you pass the Wheatsheaf Inn, where the real James Herriot and his wife spent their honeymoon.

You cannot miss Bolton Castle, which stands on a hill overlooking the valley. About two miles from Carperby, a brown heritage sign directs you up a narrow lane to the castle and the village.

The castle has dominated these surr-oundings since 1379. Round the back, by the entrance to the car-park, stands the even older St Oswald's church, compl-etely dwarfed by its neighbour. You can tell that it predated the castle – look at the sundial at midday and you will find it is in shadow!

The castle is really a massively ex-tended and fortified manor house, built by Richard le Scrope, Lord Chancellor to Richard II. It has a huge five-storey tower at each corner and turrets in the middle of each longer side. It took 18 years to com-plete, using local stone and oak timbers from the Lake District, and cost £12,000. Mary Queen of Scots was imprisoned here for six months in 1568, and in 1645 the castle was besieged by Cromwell's army, who rendered it virtually uninha-

bitable. In 1761 one of the towers blew down in a storm.

The castle, from which the village takes it name, has appeared many times in the Herriot television series; it was here, for example, that James – played by Christopher Timothy – proposed to Helen.

ON TO ASKRIGG

After that exciting detour, go back to the T-junction on the far side of Carperby and continue straight on, following the signs for *Askrigg* and *Hawes*. This is a very pretty, tree-lined road and after a couple of miles you get a lovely view of Wensleydale and Ingleborough. Eventually, four and a half miles from Carperby, you arrive at Askrigg.

Entering the village, bear left (*Hawes*) to go through the centre. There are some rather fine and unspoilt Georgian terraced houses in Askrigg, and Cringley

House, opposite St Oswald's church, may look familiar; it starred as Skeldale House, James Herriot's surgery, in *All Creatures Great and Small*. At the King's Arms Hotel, which became 'The Drovers' Arms', the bar is decorated with photographs showing the making of the series. The film-set of the surgery is on display at the Richmondshire Museum in Richmond, which is visited during the tenth tour.

ASKRIGG TO HAWES

Half a mile out of Askrigg there is a turning for *Bainbridge*. Go left here and across the River Ure to another attractive Dales village.

The Romans built a fort, called Virosidium on Brough Hill, to the east of Bainbridge, but the village owes its existence to the Normans. In the twelfth century they established it as the administrative centre for the Forest and Manor of Bainbridge.

Overlooking the green is the Rose and Crown Inn. Purely in the interests of scientific inquiry, you may feel compelled to go into the pub and investigate the Hunting Horn. Throughout the Middle Ages, from Holyrood (at the end of September) to Shrove Tuesday, the horn was blown to guide travellers out of the forest. The horn blower stood in the middle of the village green and gave three blasts at nine o'clock every night. The tradition is still upheld, though the original horn is now in the museum at Bolton Castle.

Bainbridge takes its name from the River Bain, which flows down from the fells above the village. Its source is Semer Water, the largest natural lake in Yorkshire – all 80 acres of it – and the Bain's two-mile descent makes it the shortest named river in England.

Drive through the village, and the signs for *Hawes* will bring you to the A684. Turn right and follow the road back to Hawes.

Hawes is at the heart of the Dales, and is one of its most popular villages. Despite sitting in Wensleydale, it is Yorkshire's highest market town and the second highest in England (you'll have to investigate Tour Eight if you want to visit the highest).

This route is very interesting for its Herriot connections, most of which come from the BBC television series rather than the vet himself. The real James Herriot lives and works in Thirsk, which is actually closer to the North York Moors than the Dales. However, many of his stories are set in the Dales area. When the BBC came to look for a model for his fictional village of Darrowby, they chose Askrigg, and if you visit the bar of the King's Arms, in Main Street, you can see photographs taken during filming of the television series.

Despite all this attention, there are still quiet, unspoilt areas, where you can get away from the coach parties. Heading out of Hawes via Gayle, you soon find yourself in open countryside. The road over Oughtershaw and along Langstrothdale is sufficiently steep and adventurous to ensure that you will encounter little traffic.

When researching this tour, we nearly took the route through Hardraw, to visit the famous waterfall at Hardraw Scar. At the last minute, however, we diverted through Bainbridge and discovered a very pretty little village with a lot of character. It is still worth finding the waterfall, however, but wait until you've completed the route before taking the detour. This 100ft cascade is very impressive after heavy rain and is England's highest, single drop waterfall situated above ground. Blondin, the famous nineteenth-century tightrope walker, crossed the waterfall on a tightrope. It must have been good practice for his crossing of Niagara Falls!

Cringley House, Askrigg.

TOUR FIFTEEN
~
The Forest of Bowland

The Forest of Bowland is perfect driving country. It has quiet roads, lovely views, pretty villages to explore, and it is not an area easily accessible to the walker, so you don't even need to feel guilty about seeing it from the car. It is a fascinating area, full of contrasts. It is also relatively undiscovered and an excellent escape from the tourist centres of the Lakes and Dales.

Kirkby Lonsdale to High Bentham, then over the Forest of Bowland to Slaidburn and Dunsop Bridge and along the Trough of Bowland to Quernmore, returning via Claughton and Hornby.

Distance: 55 miles. Driving time: 3 hours

Devil's Bridge, Kirkby Lonsdale.
One of the oldest stone bridges in Britain.

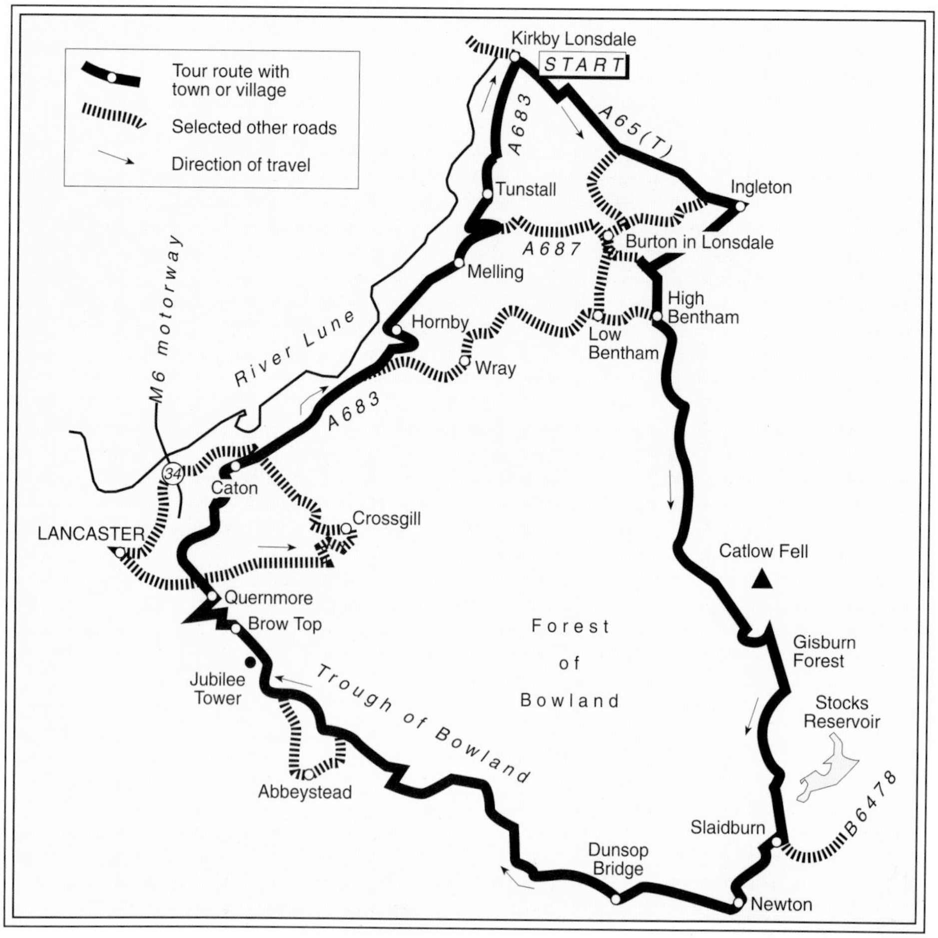
Tour route with town or village
Selected other roads
Direction of travel
Kirkby Lonsdale
START
A683
A65(T)
Ingleton
Tunstall
A687
Burton in Lonsdale
Melling
High Bentham
Hornby
Low Bentham
Wray
River Lune
M6 motorway
A683
34
Caton
Crossgill
LANCASTER
Quernmore
Brow Top
Catlow Fell
Forest of Bowland
Gisburn Forest
Jubilee Tower
Trough of Bowland
Stocks Reservoir
Abbeystead
B6478
Slaidburn
Dunsop Bridge
Newton

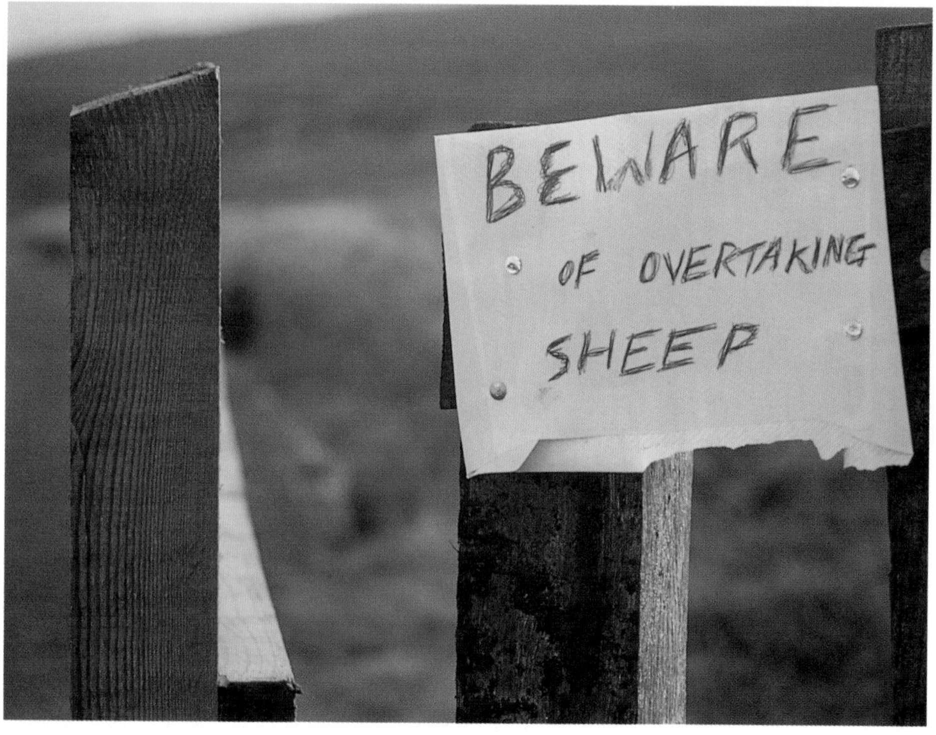
BEWARE
OF OVERTAKING
SHEEP

Left: The Forest of Bowland is grazing country for a little-known breed of experimental sheep, raised near Sellafield and capable of over 70 miles per hour over level ground.

Kirkby Lonsdale

Kirkby Lonsdale is a popular and attractive market town. There has been a market here since the thirteenth century. Market Square is not the original (it was built in 1832), but you can still see the old market cross in a little square off Market Street, just below the church.

St Mary's church is impressive, part Norman and built on the site of an earlier, Anglo-Saxon church. Look out for the distinctive rise and fall hinges as you go through the iron gates. The church backs on to a landscaped terrace known as Ruskin's View, which overlooks the River Lune and Underley Hall. Ruskin called the view 'one of the loveliest in England and therefore the world' – perhaps largely because Turner painted it.

From the terrace there is a footpath leading down to Devil's Bridge. This lovely stone bridge is one of the oldest in England and was built in the fourteenth century by monks from St Mary's Abbey, York. Bridge-building was a common activity for monks of the period, and if a bridge was built using monastery funds – rather than alms raised specifically for the purpose – it was often called Devil's Bridge.

Kirkby Lonsdale to High Bentham

The tour starts from the car-park in Market Place, in the centre of town. Turn left, down Main Street, past a number of rather fine Georgian terraced houses, to the main road, and turn left (*Skipton* and *Ingleton*), on to the A65. You can see Devil's Bridge on your left and, if you're driving past on a Sunday, you'll also see most of the Western Hemisphere's motorbike population clustered round a van serving hot snacks.

This road was originally a turnpike, built in 1751, linking Kendal and Skipton. Half a mile into Lancashire you pass the Whoop Hall Inn and go through

Right: Underley Hall and the River Lune, seen from Ruskin's View at St Mary's Church. Turner painted this scene in 1822. Below: The Great Stone of Fourstones.

Cowan Bridge. In the early nineteenth century there was a Clergy Daughters' School in the village and amongst its pupils were the Brontë sisters; Charlotte later used the countryside as a setting for her novel, *Jane Eyre*.

After five and a half miles, you approach Ingleton (by now probably convinced this is a tour to Skipton). Keep on the A65, past the first turnings for Ingleton and Burton-in-Kendal, and once you are across the iron bridge over the River Greta, look out for the turning on the right to *Bentham*, just before the Bridge Hotel. This takes you on to a pleasant, tree-lined minor road, and above the fields you can see the moors of Bowland Forest. Here, much more than in either the Lakes or Dales, you feel you are in prosperous farming country, run as big business. Look out for Volvo estate cars.

The road meanders across the fields and you catch sight of the Greta and the church spire at Burton-in-Lonsdale. Keep on the main road and after two and a half miles you come to High Bentham.

HIGH BENTHAM TO SLAIDBURN

At the T-junction with the main street, opposite the Royal Oak Sale Room, turn right and then almost immediately left, just past the Black Bull Hotel (*Slaidburn*). This narrow street takes you downhill, over the River Wenning and out of the village. The road climbs again and you are now crossing into the Forest of Bowland. Once over a cattle grid, you are out on open moor.

There are notices warning against casually wandering off the road. This is a grouse shooting moor, and public access is restricted. However, as you drive slowly uphill, look out for a large rock in the field on your right. There is a small lay-by and an opportunity for a muddy walk.

You can find the footpath easily

137

Left: The River Hodder, looking towards Dunsop Bridge with Mellor Knoll and Totridge in the background. Opposite: The memorial in the churchyard at St Hubert's.

enough because it is marked by boardwalks, to get you over the boggier patches. This boulder is the Great Stone of Fourstones (that being the name of the nearby farm), a wonderfully weathered, 15ft high lump of millstone grit. There are some steps cut into the side, and from the top the view opens out to Ingleborough and the Dales, back the way you came, and ahead to Tatham Fell and Burn Moor.

Continue over the moor for another couple of miles, then over a cattle grid and you have fields on either side. After crossing the beck at Moor Cock you then climb up on to the Tatham Fells. The road takes you past a group of sheep pens – which must be a marvellous sight when full of sheep – and then starts to wind its way up Whitray Fell. You go over a series of tiny becks which have cut great black scars through the surrounding peat moor.

You climb to another cattle grid (the third so far) by a line of wooden fencing and a sign which welcomes you to *Ribble Valley*. At this point, you can see into the valley ahead and glimpse Stocks Reservoir and Gisburn Forest, with Catlow Fell the green escarpment to the left. Just before you cross the cattle grid, look out for a large, square rock on the left; this is all that remains of the Cross of Greet, a monastic guide post. You can see the square socket on the top, where the cross stood, and there is some faint, indecipherable carving on one of the faces.

Once over the cattle grid, you start to descend. You can see the road winding down the side of Catlow Fell and in the valley below is the River Hodder, an energetic mountain beck which has just started its journey to join the River Ribble at Clitheroe. Look out for Pendle, the distinctive, flat-topped fell which you can see in the distance.

This is quite a steep gradient, so take it carefully. There are not many passing places and there is an abrupt drop on one side of the road and a ditch on the other. If you get the chance, look out for the miniature oxbow lake forming in the river below, just as you go over another cattle grid.

The road drops to cross the Hodder via the Cross of Greet Bridge, and then everything goes dark as you plunge through a small conifer wood. As you emerge, you're climbing again and have a good view of the reservoir and Gisburn Forest.

The River Hodder emerges from the southern end of Stocks Reservoir, and as you approach Slaidburn there is a really pretty view as it is joined by the River Croasdale, just as you come in sight of the village. The road takes you over the Croasdale, into Slaidburn and up to a T-junction, opposite a war memorial. Instead of going straight on for Lancaster and the Trough of Bowland, follow the road to the left (*Settle* and *Gisburn Forest*), which leads down to the river, and find the car-park by the bridge.

SLAIDBURN TO DUNSOP BRIDGE

Slaidburn is a pretty village, worth exploring on foot. There is a small café by the river and a lovely green river bank, if you have remembered to bring a picnic.

The village centre is quite small and neat, but the feature which immediately draws the eye is the name of the pub – The Hark to Bounty. This is a former coaching inn, dating back to the thirteenth century, which was originally known as The Dog. Then in 1875, the village squire called in for a drink whilst out hunting, leaving his hounds baying outside. The squire's favourite, Bounty, could be heard above all the others, and he said . . .

The inn is also notable because it contains a courtroom. This is not a

One of the owners of Hornby Castle was Sir Edward Stanley, the hero of the Battle of Flodden Field, in 1513. It remained in the Stanley family until it fell to the Roundheads in 1643, during the Civil War.

measure to improve efficiency in dealing with drink driving offences; it was once the only courtroom between York and Lancaster and was used by travelling justices up until 1937.

From the car-park, drive back to the war memorial and follow the road left (*Clitheroe, Lancaster, Trough of Bowland* and *Whitwell*). After a mile of pleasant countryside, you come to the village of Newton. Keep straight, following the signs for *Dunsop Bridge* and *Trough of Bowland*, which takes you off the B6478 and on to a minor road. Two miles later you come into Dunsop Bridge.

The village clusters around the pretty bridge over the River Dunsop, with another nice village green right beside the river. Carry on uphill to the war memorial and then turn right (*Lancaster* and *Trough of Bowland*); be careful here because the main road bears round to the left, which restricts visibility somewhat.

Half a mile later you encounter St Hubert's church, which has a 10ft high marble angel in the grounds. It is a memorial to John Townley, who had the church built when his racehorse won the Derby in 1861.

THE TROUGH OF BOWLAND

Out of Dunsop Bridge, the road climbs gradually and you pass the North West Water works at Langden Intake. This is a popular picnic area (there will probably be an ice cream van parked by the road) and is the starting-point for a walk along the beck to the ruins of Langden Castle, at the head of the valley.

Continue driving, and once you pass the seventeenth-century Sykes Farm, you have entered the Trough of Bowland. The road climbs a 17% gradient between Whins Brow, on your right, and Top of Blaze Moss. The fells are covered in bracken, gorse and heather, and in

autumn the colours can be spectacular. Once through the Trough, you descend to a pretty stretch of woodland beside the river. Look out for the bee hives. If you leave the car and take a stroll, be warned: this is a Sunday drive sort of place, which means it is also the haunt of Sunday car thieves.

As you drive through the beech trees, you pass the ivy-covered Tower Lodge on your right and shortly afterwards start encountering pheasants, all of which seem to think that they personally own the road.

The road is very level along here and you lose all sense of the surrounding fells. You pass the first road junction since Dunsop Bridge (a turning for Scorton and Garstang) and then a couple of farms. This is a very pleasant, undemanding section of the route. You pass the turning for Abbeystead and then drop again to cross Tarnbrook Wyre via a pretty humpbacked bridge. After a second bridge the road climbs Abbeystead Fell.

The view to the left gets better and better. Don't stop just yet – after a couple of miles you come to a car-park and a stone tower. Known as Jubilee Tower, it was built in 1887 by a Liverpool shipbuilder, to commemorate Queen Victoria's golden jubilee. From the top there is a wonderful panoramic view of Morecambe Bay and the surrounding countryside: Fleetwood and Blackpool are straight ahead; slightly to the right are the square buildings of Heysham nuclear power station; a little further off you can make out Lancaster and the dome of the Ashton Memorial in Williamson Park; and beyond that, across the estuary, are Grange-over-Sands, Black Combe and the Lake District fells. On a clear day you should even be able to spot the Isle of Man.

Leaving the car-park, continue downhill, past Brow Top Craft Centre and towards Quernmore.

QUERNMORE TO KIRKBY LONSDALE

As you approach the village, you want to go right at the crossroads (*Caton*), past Quernmore church (which is almost a mile from the village centre) and eventually to a T-junction. Go right towards *Caton*. As you approach the village, look out for Gresgarth Hall, on your right, with its fortified pele tower, built as a defence against the Scots in the fourteenth century. Ignore the next turning to Caton on the right and you come to another T-junction. Go right and through the village on the A683, straight across at the roundabout and you are back in farming countryside.

The River Lune flows along a wide, open valley. From time to time you can spot the river on your left. You go through the village of Claughton (pronounced 'Clafton'), and past a brick works. As you approach Hornby you can see the battlements of Hornby Castle ahead. Of the original thirteenth-century castle only the keep remains; the rest was rebuilt in the eighteenth and nineteenth centuries. It is not open to the public, but you get a good view of it as you drive through the village.

The road continues to Melling and then on to a junction with the A687. Follow the A683 left (*Kirkby Lonsdale*) and into Tunstall, another village with a privately owned castle. Thurland Castle even has a moat, but it stands in a large park and is invisible from the road. As you leave the village look out for Church Lane, on your right. Just up here is Tunstall church, which served as a model for 'Brocklebridge church' in Charlotte Brontë's *Jane Eyre*. From here you get a view of the castle.

The road enters Burrow. Or Burrow-with-Burrow, according to the road sign, although it is not very clear whether the Burrow you enter is Burrow or Burrow. You pass the Highwayman Inn, and two miles later come back to the A65.

Turn left for *Kirkby Lonsdale*, and if you want to investigate Devil's Bridge, take the turning to the right (*Sedbergh*) just before you come to the turning for Kirkby Lonsdale town centre.

Kirkby Lonsdale is a lovely market town, full of charm and character. In addition to a weekly market, there's an annual event which draws in the crowds. This is the Victorian Fair which is held in early September. Residents dress up in period costume and anyone caught in modern clothing receives a fine from a Victorian policeman! There is an old-time music hall and numerous special events so if you are here around the right time, it's worth getting details from the Kirkby Lonsdale information centre.

The drive through Bowland is good and varied. Slaidburn is a fascinating little village – like stepping back forty years in time. Don't miss the Hark to Bounty Inn, with its ancient courtroom.

One of the highspots of the tour – quite literally – is the view from Jubilee Tower. The car-park next to it is also quite interesting – not in itself, but because of what they found there when it was built. During its construction in 1973, one of the mechanical diggers unearthed a burial mound. Wrapped in a large woollen shroud were the remains of a body. In fact, very little of the body survived, but the shroud was well-preserved. Carbon analysis dated it to the early seventh century, making it one of the largest pieces of woven cloth to be found from that era. It is now on display in the Lancaster City Museum.

There's also an interesting story associated with the Shell garage, half a mile north of Claughton (just past the turning for Farleton): the story goes that in the 1920s or 1930s, the owner of the then Old Toll House Garage painted white lines on the road because of frequent accidents. After much debate, King George V recognized their value and their use became accepted practice world-wide. Although the story is well known locally, even Lancaster Museum isn't sure whether or not it is true. So if you happen to be an authority on white lines, I'm sure they would like to hear from you!

The Hark to Bounty Inn, Slaidburn.

TOURING INFORMATION

~

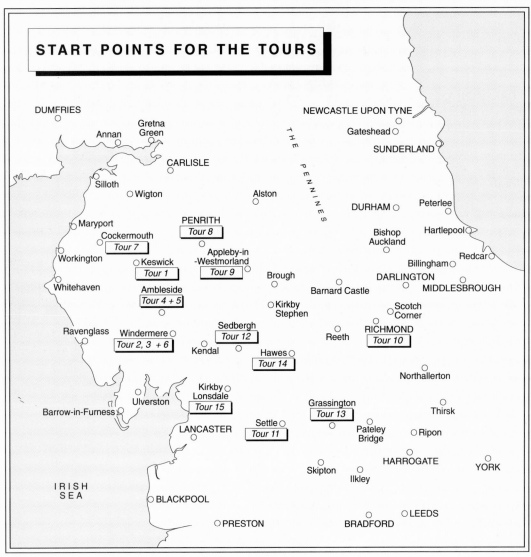

START POINTS FOR THE TOURS

DUMFRIES

Annan   Gretna
Green

CARLISLE

Silloth
Wigton   Alston

Maryport   PENRITH
Cockermouth   *Tour 8*
Tour 7   Appleby-in
Workington   -Westmorland
Keswick   *Tour 9*   Brough
Whitehaven
Ambleside
Tour 4 + 5

Ravenglass   Windermere   Sedbergh
Tour 2, 3 + 6   *Tour 12*
Kendal   Hawes
Tour 14

Kirkby
Lonsdale   Grassington
Ulverston   *Tour 15*   *Tour 13*
Barrow-in-Furness
LANCASTER   Settle   Pateley
Tour 11   Bridge

IRISH
SEA   Skipton   Ilkley
BLACKPOOL

PRESTON   BRADFORD

NEWCASTLE UPON TYNE
Gateshead
SUNDERLAND

THE PENNINES

DURHAM   Peterlee
Bishop   Hartlepool
Auckland
Redcar
Billingham
DARLINGTON
Barnard Castle   MIDDLESBROUGH

Kirkby
Stephen   Scotch
Corner
Reeth   RICHMOND
Tour 10

Northallerton

Thirsk

Ripon

HARROGATE   YORK

LEEDS

In this section you will find general information about the area, its national parks, the regional tourist boards, a complete list of tourist information centres as well as a list of other useful addresses. Following this section is information specific to each tour – the sort of thing you might find useful while on the drive or before you set off. We've included the Ordnance Survey maps which

cover the tour, plus a small selection of pubs and hotels. In choosing the recommended accommodation, we have aimed at places with character, a welcoming atmosphere and a reputation for good food and wine. It is also worth bearing in mind that in country areas such as the Lakes and Dales, many of the hotels are open to non-residents and have some of the best

restaurants in the area. Sharrow Bay and Miller Howe in the Lake District, for example, have an excellent world-wide reputation based primarily on their food.

Visitor attractions which are on the routes are also listed, plus a few additions which are worth a detour. Opening times vary, so latest details, contact the nearest tourist information centre. Note that attractions are usually closed on

Christmas day. The location of these attractions is also shown on the tour maps. The numbers on these maps refer to the corresponding numbers in the list of visitor attractions for each tour. Craft shops vary from large commercial concerns to small, friendly local enterprises. On the whole, we've concentrated on the smaller ones and given details of opening times if they are particularly idiosyncratic.

And as Stirling mentioned in his introduction, petrol stations can close very early in the country. In case of an emergency, we have listed the nearest late night fuel and emergency breakdown garages on each tour. If you come across any others or indeed any other information you think would be helpful, we would be glad to receive it for use in future editions.

TOURIST INFORMATION CENTRES

With one or two exceptions, all the following are network tourist information centres (TICs), which means that they offer a range of services, including accommodation booking. In most cases they can book accommodation outside their immediate area. National Park TICs sometimes offer these services as well as providing more general information about the history, geology and background to their areas. Some of them have excellent exhibitions and a range of publications specifically related to the National Parks. We have listed them alphabetically, by county, and marked National Park TICs with an asterisk.

(CW) *means closed in winter.*

CUMBRIA

Alston	01434 381696
Ambleside	015394 32582
Appleby	017683 51177
Barrow-in-Furness	01229 870156
Bowness-on-Windermere* (CW)	015394 42895
Brampton (CW)	016977 3433
Carlisle	01228 512444
Cockermouth	01900 822634
Coniston* (CW)	015394 41533
Egremont	01946 820693
Glenridding* (CW)	017684 82414
Grange-over-Sands (CW)	015395 34026
Grasmere* (CW)	015394 35245
Hawkshead* (CW)	015394 36525
Kendal	01539 725758
Keswick	017687 72645
Killington Lake	015396 20138
Kirkby Lonsdale	015242 71437
Kirkby Stephen	017683 71199
Longtown	01228 791876
Maryport	01900 813738
Millom	01229 772555
Penrith	01768 67466
Pooley Bridge* (CW)	017684 86530
Ravenglass (CW)	01229 717278
Seatoller* (CW)	017687 77294
Sedbergh* (CW)	015396 20125
Silloth (CW)	016973 31944
Southwaite	016974 73445/6
Ulverston	01229 587120
Whitehaven	01946 695678
Windermere	015394 46499
Workington	01900 602923

The Lake District National Park has two additional information centres:

Waterhead, Ambleside (CW)	015394 32729
Keswick Discovery Centre (CW)	017687 72803

And also runs the National Park Visitor Centre at Brockhole, Windermere, telephone 015394 46601. Open April to November.

Note: Although Sedbergh is in Cumbria, it is also in the Yorkshire Dales National Park. To foil their attempt to confuse, we've listed their TIC twice.

YORKSHIRE AND THE DALES

Aysgarth Falls* (CW)	01969 663424
Bedale (CW)	01677 24604
Bentham (CW)	015242 62549
Clapham* (CW)	015242 51419
Grassington* (CW)	01756 752774
Hawes* (CW)	01969 667450
Horton-in-Ribblesdale	017296 333
Ingleton (CW)	015242 41049
Leyburn	01969 23069
Malham* (CW)	01729 830363
Pateley Bridge (CW)	01423 711147
Richmond	01748 850222
Scotch Corner (CW)	01325 377677
Sedbergh* (CW)	015396 20125
Settle	01729 825192
Skipton	01756 792809

NORTH LANCASHIRE

Charnock Richard, M6	01257 793773
Forton Services, M6	01524 792181
Morecambe	01524 414110
Lancaster	01524 32878

NATIONAL PARKS

Lake District National Park
Brockhole, Windermere,
Cumbria, LA23 1LJ

Yorkshire Dales National Park
Colvend, Hebden Road,
Grassington, Skipton, North
Yorkshire, BD23 5LB

National Park Publications
Both the Lake District and
Yorkshire Dales have a range of publications on local walks, history and geography. They also each publish an annual newspaper, which lists events and activities within the Park and is available free from tourist information centres:
The Lake District Guardian
The Yorkshire Dales Visitor

In addition, the Lake District publishes *Events*, an annual listing of courses and activities organized by the National Park.

NATIONAL TRUST

The National Trust
The Hollens, Grasmere,
Cumbria, LA22 9QZ

The National Trust
Goddards, 27 Tadcaster Road,
Dringhouses, York, YO2 2QG

TOURISM ORGANIZATIONS

Cumbria Tourist Board
Ashleigh, Holly Road,
Windermere,
Cumbria, LA23 2AQ
Telephone 015934 44444

Yorkshire and Humberside
Tourist Board
312 Tadcastle Road,
York, YO2 2HF
Telephone 01904 707961

Lancaster Tourism
Lancaster City Council,
29 Castle Hill,
Lancaster, LA1 1YN
Telephone 01524 582902

All three publish accommodation guides and a range of booklets on walks, places to visit and things to do. The Cumbria Tourist Board also produces a very handy map – *Cumbria, The Lake District Touring Map*.

TELEPHONE WEATHER INFORMATION

Mountain areas sometimes have their own weather systems which bear no relation to the general weather predictions for a region. There are two weather line services, updated twice a day, which give specific forecasts for the National Parks. Unless you have your own seaweed, they are probably about as accurate as you can get:

Lake District   015394 45151
Run by the National Park Authority and operates throughout the year, with fell-top walking conditions in winter.

Yorkshire Dales   01891 500748
An all-year-round service operated by British Telecom, so there is an extra charge in addition to the cost of a normal call.

TOUR ONE
~
Caldbeck and John Peel Country

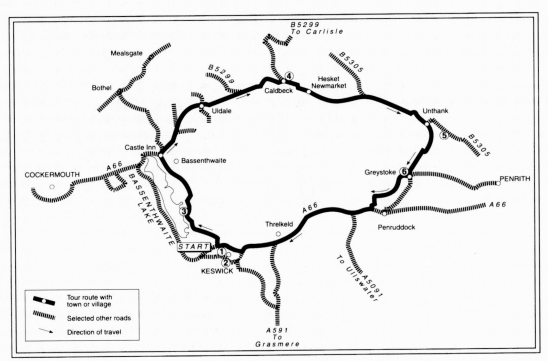

to companies interested in laying on corporate hospitality and events. Contact Douglas Weymouth for full details.

CRAFT SHOPS
Priest's Mill – see above.

Thornthwaite Galleries
Thornthwaite, Nr Keswick.
Telephone 017687 78248.
Artworks and crafts, some of them highly unusual. Nice café on site.

MARKETS
Keswick – Saturday

LATE-NIGHT FUEL
Fitz Park Service Station
Penrith Road, Keswick (on the A591). Telephone 017687 72386. Open until 8.00 pm.

24-HOUR BREAKDOWN
Ullswater Road Body Repairs
Ullswater Road, Penrith.
Telephone 01768 864546.

Neil Bousfield Motors
Cromwell Road, Penrith.
Telephone 01768 892727.

MAPS
OS Landranger no. 90
OS Touring Map 3 The Lake District

RECOMMENDED ACCOMMODATION
Pheasant Inn
Wythop Village, Bassenthwaite Lake. Telephone 017687 76234.

The Mill Hotel
Mungrisedale, Penrith.
Telephone 017687 79659.

VISITOR ATTRACTIONS
1 Cumberland Pencil Museum
Southey Works, Keswick.
Telephone 017687 73626.
The history of pencil making, from the discovery of graphite in the fells of Borrowdale to the world's largest pencil. Open all year, every day, except Christmas Day, Boxing Day and New Years' Day.

2 Cars of the Stars Museum
Standish Street, Keswick.
Telephone 017687 73757.
A delightful new museum which appeals to car and film buffs alike. Open Easter to New Year, daily.

3 Mirehouse
Bassenthwaite Lake, Keswick.
Telephone 017687 72287.
A seventeenth-century hunting lodge, and the home of the Spedding family since 1802. Some fascinating literary connections. Open Easter to October. Please note: house open on Wednesday, Sunday, bank holiday Mondays and Fridays in August only. Grounds open every day.

4 Priest's Mill
Caldbeck, Nr Wigton.
Telephone 016974 78369.
A very carefully converted

former watermill, now the home of an excellent café, bookshop and a number of other attractions. Open March to October, every day except Monday.

5 Hutton-in-the-Forest
Penrith. Telephone 017684 84449.
The home of Lord Inglewood, a rather fine mansion based around a fourteenth-century pele tower. Still a private residence, so, like Mirehouse, opening times are restricted. Open May to September: *note* Thursdays, Fridays, Sundays and bank holidays only.

6 Greystoke Castle Estate
Greystoke Castle, Penrith.
Telephone 017684 83722.
A private residence and not generally open to the public, but the castle and grounds are open

TOUR TWO
~
The Langdales and Tarn Hows

MAPS
OS Landranger nos. 90, 97
OS Touring Map 3 The Lake
District

RECOMMENDED ACCOMMODATION
Lindeth Fell Hotel
Lyth Valley Road,
Bowness-on-Windermere.
Telephone 015394 43286.

Miller Howe
Rayrigg Road,
Bowness-on-Windermere.
Telephone 015394 42536.

Three Shires Inn
Little Langdale, Nr Ambleside.
Telephone 015394 37215.

Ees Wyke
Near Sawrey, Windermere.
Telephone 015394 36393.

South Lakeland farm holidays –
Telephone 01539 823682.

VISITOR ATTRACTIONS
1 Brockhole
Lake District National Park
Visitor Centre, Windermere.
Telephone 015394 46601.
A large house in beautiful
grounds with access to the lake's
shore. It has an adventure
playground for the kids and a
regular programme of events to
keep the adults amused. Audio-
visual events take place daily.
Open April to October, every
day. Admission free. Parking
charge.

**2 The World of Beatrix
Potter**
The Old Laundry, Rayrigg
Road,
Bowness-on-Windermere.
Telephone 015394 88444.

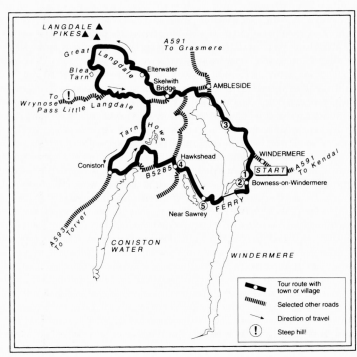

Excellent displays bring Beatrix
Potter's characters to life. Open
all year, daily.

**3 Windermere Steamboat
Museum**
Rayrigg Road,
Bowness-on-Windermere.
Telephone 015394 45565.
An impressive collection of old
steam craft. Two of the steam
launches make regular passenger
trips on the lake. Open Easter to
October, daily.

4 Hill Top
Near Sawrey, Windermere.
Telephone 015394 36269.
Beatrix Potter's famous Lake
District home. Open Easter to
October, Saturday to Wednesday
only. Gardens and shop open
seven days a week.

CRAFT SHOPS
Made in Cumbria

Tourist Information Centre,
Windermere.
Telephone 015394 46499.
A range of local crafts.

Crafts at Barnhowe
Lane Ends, Elterwater, Langdale.
Telephone 015394 37346.
Spinning and weaving.

The Craftsman's Loft
Church Hill, Hawkshead.
Telephone 015394 36312.
Local north-west arts and crafts.

BOAT TRIPS
Windermere Lake Cruises
Lakeside, Nr Ulverston.
Telephone 015395 31188.
The original Windermere
launches; they run regular
services throughout the day and
provide a magnificent way to see
the lake and surrounding
countryside. The service runs all
year, except Christmas Day.

MARKETS
Ambleside – Wednesday

LATE-NIGHT FUEL
Rayrigg Motors
Rayrigg Road,
Bowness-on-Windermere.
Telephone 015394 42716.
Open until 9.00 pm.

Hill's Garage
Lake Road, Ambleside.
Telephone 015394 32144.
Open until 11.00 pm.

24-HOUR BREAKDOWN
Young Motors
Knott Street, Ambleside.
Telephone 015394 32322.

Ullswater Road Garage
West Moorland Business Park,
off Shepp Road, Kendal.
Telephone 01539 730730.

TOUR THREE
~
Ullswater and Borrowdale

MAPS
OS Landranger nos. 89, 90
OS Touring Map 3 The Lake District

RECOMMENDED ACCOMMODATION
Leeming House Hotel
Watermillock, Ullswater.
Telephone 017684 86622.

Old Church Hotel
Watermillock, Ullswater.
Telephone 017684 86204.

Sharrow Bay Country House Hotel
Howtown, Ullswater.
Telephone 017684 86301.

Swinside Lodge Hotel
Stair, Newlands, Keswick.
Telephone 017687 72948.

Rampsbeck Country House Hotel
Watermillock, Ullswater.
Telephone 017684 86442.

VISITOR ATTRACTIONS
1 Lakeland Horticultural Society Garden
Holehird, Patterdale Road (A592),
Windermere.
Telephone 015394 46008.
An attractive garden and grounds. Open all year, every day. Free admission.

2 Townend
Troutbeck, Windermere.
Telephone 015394 32628.
Owned by the National Trust and probably their finest house open to the public in the Lake District. Open Easter to October, Tuesday to Friday and Sunday, 1–5 pm (last admission 4.30).

3 Cars of the Stars – see Tour One

4 Cumberland Pencil Museum – see Tour One.

5 Seatoller Barn
Seatoller, Borrowdale.
Telephone 017687 77294.
In addition to being a National Park information centre, this is also a good exhibition of local crafts. Open April to October.

6 Whinlatter Visitor Centre
Whinlatter Pass, Braithwaite, Keswick.
Telephone 017687 78469.
An excellent and recently revamped forest visitor centre. Open all year except January.

7 Dove Cottage
Town End, Grasmere.
Telephone 015394 35544.
William Wordsworth's most

famous home. He lived here whilst at the height of his powers. Open all year, except mid-January to mid-February.

8 Rydal Mount and Garden
Rydal, Nr Ambleside.
Telephone 015394 33002.
Wordsworth's last home; he died here in 1850. Open all year except late January, every day except Tuesdays in winter.

CRAFT SHOPS
Adrian Sankey
Rydal Road, Ambleside.
Telephone 015394 33039.
Glassware, blown on site, and decorative lighting.

Seatoller Barn – see Visitor Attractions.

BOAT TRIPS
Ullswater Navigation and Transit Company

Glenridding Pier, Glenridding, Ullswater.
Telephone 017684 82229.
Note that there is an excellent walk if you get off half-way – at Howtown – and walk the seven miles back along the shore to Glenridding. The service runs Easter to September, every day; reduced service in October.

Keswick on Derwent Launch Company
Lake Side, Keswick.
Telephone 017687 72263.
An excellent way to link up a boat ride with a walk along the shore. Service runs all year.

MARKETS
Ambleside – Wednesday
Keswick – Saturday

LATE-NIGHT FUEL
Hill's Garage
Lake Road, Ambleside.
Telephone 015394 32144.
Open until 11.00 pm.

Fitz Park Service Station
Penrith Road, Keswick (on the A591). Telephone 017687 72386.
Open until 8.00 pm.

24-HOUR BREAKDOWN
Young Motors
Knott Street, Ambleside.
Telephone 015394 32322.

Ullswater Road Garage
Ullswater Road, Penrith.
Telephone 01768 64546.

TOUR FOUR
~
The Western Lakes

MAPS
OS Landranger nos. 89, 90
OS Touring Map 3 The Lake District

RECOMMENDED ACCOMMODATION
Lakeside Hotel
Thirlmere.
Telephone 017687 72478.

Pickett Howe
Brackenthwaite, Buttermere Valley,
Cockermouth.
Telephone 01900 85444.
A very nice converted farm, though quite small.

VISITOR ATTRACTIONS
1 Hardknott Roman Fort
Hardknott Pass.
A magnificent Roman fort. The brilliant view must have been some compensation for the legionaries stationed here during the long Cumbrian winters. Open all year, free access.

2 Eskdale Corn Mill
Boot, Eskdale.
Telephone 019467 23335.
Small, converted corn mill. No longer a working mill but has a good display on its history and technology. Open April to September, every day except Saturday (open bank holiday Saturdays).

3 Muncaster Castle
Muncaster, Ravenglass.
Telephone 01229 717614.
Originally a pele tower, now a large mansion set in magnificent grounds, famous for rhododendrons and azaleas. There is also a small zoo and this is now the home of the British Owl Breeding and Release

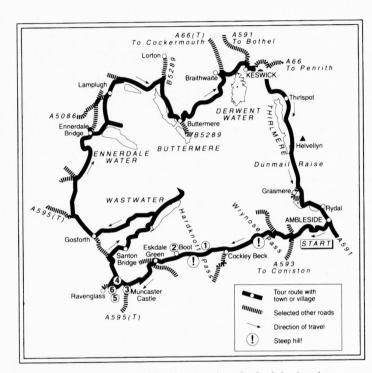

Centre. Castle open mid-March to early November, Sunday to Friday 12.30–4.00 pm. (Grounds and Owl Centre open every day.)

4 Muncaster Water Mill
Ravenglass.
Telephone 01229 717232.
A working corn mill in regular use and one of the stops for the Ravenglass and Eskdale Railway. Freshly produced flour available. Open daily April to October and weekends in winter.

5 Ravenglass & Eskdale Railway
Ravenglass.
Telephone 01229 717171.
'La'al Ratty' to the locals, this narrow-gauge railway was once a mining line but is now run for the benefit of passengers. It follows a scenic route around the northern flanks of Muncaster Fell. The service runs all year, but with

reduced schedules in winter.

6 Walls Castle
Roman Bath House, Ravenglass.
A surprisingly intact Roman bath-house, once associated with the Roman fort at Ravenglass. It is hidden in the trees behind the village but there is a pleasant walk towards it. Open all year.

For Keswick attractions, Dove Cottage and Rydal Mount, see Tours One and Three.

CRAFT CENTRES
Fold End Gallery
Boot, Eskdale.
Telephone 019467 23213.
Sells original watercolours and oil paintings.

Gosforth Pottery
Gosforth.
Telephone 019467 25296.
Open all year, except Mondays,

Tuesdays and Wednesdays throughout January to March.

Lowes Court Gallery
12 Main Street, Egremont.
Telephone 01946 820693.
Supports arts and crafts from West Cumbria, with exhibitions, displays and sales.

MARKETS
Ambleside – Wednesday
Keswick – Saturday

LATE-NIGHT FUEL
Hill's Garage
Lake Road, Ambleside.
Telephone 015394 32144.
Open until 11.00 pm.

Fitz Park Service Station
Penrith Road, Keswick (on the A591). Telephone 017687 72386. Open until 8.00 pm.

Pelican Self-Service Garage
Loop Road North, Whitehaven.
Telephone 01946 66363.
Open 24 hours.

Oakhirst Service Station
Lamplugh Road, Cockermouth.
Telephone 01900 823316. Open until 11.00 pm.

24-HOUR BREAKDOWN
Young Motors
Knott Street, Ambleside.
Telephone 015394 32322.

R. and A. Postlethwaite
Fell View Garage
Eskdale Green, Eskdale.
Telephone 019467 23239 or 23317.

Frizington Motors
Main Street, Frizington.
Telephone 01946 811036 (day), 01946 810764 (night).

TOUR FIVE
~
The Duddon Valley

MAPS
OS Landranger nos. 96, 97
OS Touring Map 3 The Lake
District

**RECOMMENDED
ACCOMMODATION**
Rothay Manor Hotel
Ambleside.
Telephone 015394 33605.

Appletree Holme
Blawith, Coniston.
Telephone 01229 885618.

VISITOR ATTRACTIONS
1 Brantwood
Coniston.
Telephone 015394 41396.
Ruskin's home, one of the most
beautifully-sited houses in
England. Excellent nature trail
around the grounds and usually a
range of events and special
exhibitions throughout the year.
The café is excellent. Open
March to November, every day;
November to March, Wednesday
to Sunday only.

2 Grizedale Forest Visitor Centre
Grizedale Forest, Satterthwaite.
Telephone 01229 860010.
Slightly off the main tour but
worth a diversion. Fascinating
exhibition, recently revamped.
The forest itself is open all year
and there are numerous way-
marked footpaths and trails. Look
out for the Forest Sculptures;
bold, imaginative creations using
natural materials which blend into
the landscape. Visitor Centre
open all year: low season 10 am–5
pm; high season 10 am–5.30 pm;
January and February 11 am–4
pm. 7 days a week.

3 Wray Castle
Low Wray, Ambleside.

Telephone 015394 40200.
This is not on the tour but if you
happen to be on the east side of
Lake Windermere, looking
north, you may spot a strange
castle, lurking in the trees on the
north-west shore. It is a Victorian
folly, built over 150 years ago.
Owned by the National Trust
and now used by the Merchant
Navy as a marine electronics
College (the only one of its kind
in the world). The grounds are
open daily and a public footpath
leads past the castle and along
the lake's shore. A highly
recommended afternoon stroll.
The castle is not open to the
public.

CRAFT SHOPS
The Coach House Gallery
Brantwood, Coniston.
Telephone 015394 41426.
An excellent, high quality range
of arts and crafts, displayed in

the rooms above the Jumping
Jenny Tea Room.

BOAT TRIPS
Gondola Steam Launch
Coniston.
Telephone 015394 41288.
Regular sailings, daily from April
to October.

MARKETS
Ambleside – Wednesday

LATE-NIGHT FUEL
Hill's Garage
Lake Road, Ambleside.
Telephone 015394 32144.
Open until 11.00 pm.

Furness Park Services
Abbey Road, Barrow-in-Furness.
Telephone 01229 820595.
Open 24 hours.

24-HOUR BREAKDOWN
Young Motors

Knott Street, Ambleside.
Telephone 015394 32322.

H.H. Miller & Son
38 The Gill, Ulverston.
Telephone 01229 582057 (day),
01229 585201 (night).

48

TOUR SIX

~

Cartmel and the Winster Valley

MAPS
OS Landranger no. 97

RECOMMENDED ACCOMMODATION
Aynsome Manor Hotel
Cartmel, Nr Grange-over-Sands.
Telephone 015395 36653.

The Old Vicarage
Church Road, Witherslack.
Telephone 015395 52381.

Uplands Hotel
Haggs Lane, Cartmel,
Grange-over-Sands.
Telephone 015395 36248.

VISITOR ATTRACTIONS
1 Stott Park Bobbin Mill
Finsthwaite, Newby Bridge.
Telephone 015395 31087.
A working bobbin mill right up
until 1971, re-opened as a
museum in 1983. You can see
much of the original machinery
and there are guided tours and
demonstrations. A unique
venture, well worth seeking out.
Open April to October, every
day.

2 Lakeside and Haverthwaite
Railway
Haverthwaite.
Telephone 015395 31594.
Part of the line which once ran
from Lakeside to Ulverston, now
run by enthusiasts, with steam
trains connecting Haverthwaite
with the boats at Lakeside. Runs
from Easter to early November.

3 Cartmel Priory Church
Cartmel.
Open every day, free.

The next two attractions are
slightly off the tour, but in view
of the nature of one of them we

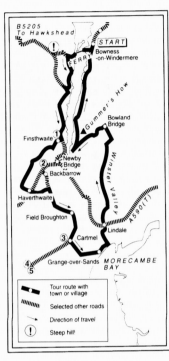

could hardly fail to mention
them:

4 Holker Hall
Cark-in-Cartmel,
Nr Grange-over-Sands.
A magnificent seventeenth-
century country house, home of
the Cavendish family and set in
park land which once belonged
to Cartmel Priory. In addition to
the house and grounds, events
are held throughout the year,
such as model aeroplane rallies,
hot air ballooning, MG rallies, so
it's worth getting their
programme of events. Open
April to October, every day
except Saturday.

5 Lakeland Motor Museum
Holker Hall, Cark-in-Cartmel,
Nr Grange-over-Sands.
Telephone 015395 58509.
In the grounds of Holker Hall,
the Lakeland Motor Museum is a

sort of northern Beaulieu with
over 80 historic vehicles plus a
replica of Donald Campbell's
Bluebird used in the BBC TV
play. The entrance fee is in
addition to the charge to visit
Holker Hall. Open April to
October, every day except
Saturday.

CRAFT SHOPS
Lyth Gallery
Town Yeat, Underbarrow.
Telephone 015395 68383.
Houses a range of works of art.

BOAT TRIPS
Windermere Iron Steamboat
Company – see Tour Two.

LATE-NIGHT FUEL
Newby Bridge Motors
Newby Bridge.
Telephone 015395 31253.
Open until 10.00 pm.

Rayrigg Motors
Rayrigg Road,
Bowness-on-Windermere.
Telephone 015394 42716.
Open until 9.00 pm.

24-HOUR BREAKDOWN
James Atkinson & Son Ltd
Canal Garage, Crooklands,
Milnthorpe.
Telephone 015395 67401.

Crooklands Mill Garage
Crooklands, Milnthorpe.
Telephone 015395 67216.

Crooklands Motor Company
Crooklands, Milnthorpe.
Telephone 015395 67414.

Hargreaves Garages
Sandes Avenue, Kendal.
Telephone 01539 724420.

TOUR SEVEN
~
Cockermouth and the Solway Coast

MAPS
OS Landranger nos. 85, 89, 90

RECOMMENDED ACCOMMODATION

The Beeches
Wood Street, Carlisle.
Telephone 01228 511962.

The Crown
Wetherall, Near Carlisle.
Telephone 01228 561888.

Crosby Lodge Hotel
Crosby-on-Eden.
Telephone 01228 573618.

VISITOR ATTRACTIONS

1 Wordsworth House
Main Street, Cockermouth.
Telephone 01900 824805.
The house where Wordsworth
and his sister, Dorothy, were
born. A fine Georgian mansion
with a splendid garden and a nice
café on site. Open April to
October, weekdays only and
Saturdays in August.

2 The Printing Museum
102 Main Street, Cockermouth.
Telephone 01900 824984.
A small, privately-run collection
of old printing blocks and
machines. Open all year, every
day except Sunday.

3 Cumberland Toy and Model
Museum
Bank's Court, Market Place,
Cockermouth.
Telephone 01900 827606.
Features a range of toys from
1900 to the present. Open
February to November, every
day.

4 Jennings Brewery Tours
Jennings Brewery, Brewery Lane,
Cockermouth.

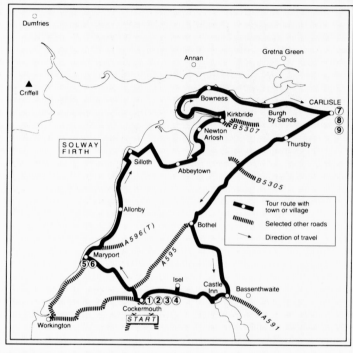

Telephone 01900 823214.
Tours available from February to
November, Monday to Friday at
11 am and 2 pm.

5 Maryport Maritime Museum
1 Senhouse Street, Maryport.
Telephone 01900 813738.
A small exhibition housed in the
tourist information centre with
some fascinating displays about
Maryport's long maritime
history. Open Easter to October,
every day; the rest of the year,
closed on Sundays.

6 Maryport Steamship
Museum
Elizabeth Dock, Maryport
Harbour.
Telephone 01900 815954.
A pair of real steamships which
you can wander around and
explore. Open Easter to
October, every day except
Thursday.

7 Senhouse Roman Museum
The Battery, Sea Brows,
Maryport.
Telephone 01900 816168.
A collection of Roman relics
brought together by the
Senhouse family. Open
November to March, Friday to
Sunday; April, June and
October, closed Mondays and
Wednesdays; the rest of the year,
open daily.

8 Tullie House Museum and Art
Gallery
Castle Street, Carlisle.
Telephone 01228 34781.
An excellent, recently
refurbished museum chronicling
the history of Cumbria and the
Borders. Open daily throughout
the year. Ground floor and art
gallery, admission free.

9 Border Regiment Museum
Queen Mary Tower, Carlisle

Castle, Carlisle.
Telephone 01228 32774.
Open every day throughout the
year.

10 Guild Hall Museum
Nr Old Town Hall, Carlisle.
Telephone 01228 34781.
Open Easter to September only.
Telephone for opening times.

MARKETS

Carlisle – indoor market
Monday to Saturday, except
Thursday pm.
Cockermouth – Monday
Silloth – Sunday

LATE-NIGHT FUEL

Oakhirst Service Station
Lamplugh Road, Cockermouth.
Telephone 01900 823316.
Open until 11.00 pm.

Essex Garage
Maryport Road, Dearham.
Telephone 01900 814374.
Open until 10.00 pm.

Brunton Park Service Station
Warwick Road, Carlisle.
Telephone 01228 28715.
Open until midnight.

Harraby Green Service Station
London Road, Carlisle.
Telephone 01228 20973.
Open 24 hours.

24-HOUR BREAKDOWN

Carleton Service Station
London Road, Carleton, Carlisle.
Telephone 01228 27287.

DMK Auto Electrics
4/5 Currock Trade Centre,
Currock Road, Carlisle.
Telephone 01228 512438.

TOUR EIGHT
~
Alston and Hadrian's Wall

MAPS

OS Landranger nos. 86, 90, 91

RECOMMENDED ACCOMMODATION

Kirby Moor Hotel
Longtown Road, Brampton.
Telephone 016977 3893.

Lovelady Shield Country House Hotel
Nenthall, Alston.
Telephone 01434 381203.

Loaning Head House
Garrigill, Alston.
Telephone 01434 381013.
A good vegetarian guest house.

Eden Valley and Alston Moor – Farm holidays
Telephone 016974 76230.

Hadrian's Wall farm holidays – there is a useful leaflet available from Carlisle or Brampton TIC or the Cumbria Tourist Board.

VISITOR ATTRACTIONS

1 Nunnery Walks
Nunnery House Hotel, Staffield, Kirkoswald, Penrith.
Telephone 01768 898537.
Delightful walk along the River Eden, through Eden Gorge.
Open all year.

2 Talkin Tarn
Nr Brampton. Telephone Cumbria County Council on 016977 3129. Pleasant tarn and country park. Free access.

3 Naworth Castle
Brampton. Telephone 016977 3229.
Stately home of the Howard family, dating back to 1335. Note restricted opening times: Easter weekend, then during May to

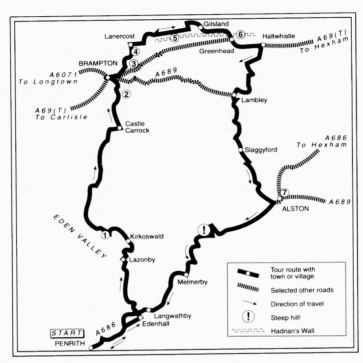

September, Wednesday and Sunday only; also Saturdays in July and August.

4 Lanercost Church and Ruins
Brampton.
Telephone 016977 73030.
Open in the summer only.

5 Birdoswald Roman Fort
Gilsland, Nr Brampton.
Telephone 016977 47602.
Open Easter to October, daily.

6 The Roman Army Museum
Carvoran, Greenhead, Carlisle.
Telephone 016977 47485.
Open March to October, every day; November and February, weekends only; closed December and January.

7 South Tynedale Railway
Alston.
Telephone 01434 381696.
Service runs at Easter, spring

weekends; September and October – every day except Monday and Friday; June – Thursdays only; July and August – daily; November – Sundays only; closed December to Easter. Leaflets are available from Brampton and Alston tourist information centres.

CRAFT SHOPS

Eden Craft Gallery
St Andrew's Churchyard, Penrith. Telephone 01768 867955.
Locally made crafts.

Gossipgate Gallery
The Butts, Alston.
Telephone 01434 381806.

The Village Bakery
Melmerby, Penrith.
Telephone 01768 881515.
Nice range of locally made crafts

for sale, as well as locally produced bread and cakes.

MARKETS

Brampton – Wednesday
Penrith – Tuesday and Saturday

LATE-NIGHT FUEL

Davidson's Garage
Scotland Road, Penrith.
Telephone 01768 862456.
Open until midnight.

24-HOUR BREAKDOWN

Eden Garage
Temple Sowerby, Nr Penrith.
Telephone 017683 61212.

Ullswater Road Garage
Ullswater Road, Penrith.
Telephone 01768 64546.

Neil Bousfield Motors
Cromwell Road, Penrith.
Telephone 01768 67808.

TOUR NINE
~
The Villages of the Eden

MAPS
OS Landranger nos. 90, 91

RECOMMENDED ACCOMMODATION
Temple Sowerby House Hotel
Temple Sowerby, Appleby-in-Westmorland.
Telephone 017683 61578.

Appleby Manor Country House Hotel
Roman Road, Appleby-in-Westmorland.
Telephone 017683 51571.

Tufton Arms Hotel
Market Square, Appleby-in-Westmorland.
Telephone 017683 51593.

VISITOR ATTRACTIONS
1 Appleby Castle
Appleby-in-Westmorland.
Telephone 017683 51402.
Beautifully preserved castle and extensive earthworks set in 27 acres of riverside grounds.
Open Easter to October, every day.

2 Lowther Leisure and Wildlife Park
Hackthorpe, Penrith.
Telephone 01931 712523.
Large parkland with deer-park, narrow-gauge railway and a small family circus. Open Easter to Spring Bank Holiday, weekends only; then daily to mid-September.

3 Lakeland Bird of Prey Centre
Lowther Park, Hackthorpe, Penrith.
Telephone 01931 712746.
A breeding and training centre for falcons, with displays all year round. Open all year, daily.

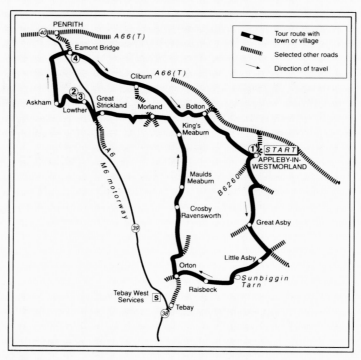

4 Brougham Castle
Brougham, Penrith.
Telephone 01768 862488.
Open April to October, daily.

CRAFT SHOPS
Brougham Hall
Brougham, Penrith.
Telephone 01768 868184.
In order to rescue the Hall from dereliction, there are now craft centres selling local crafts on site. There is a small admission charge. Open all year, daily.

Wetheriggs Pottery
Clifton Dykes, Penrith.
Telephone 01768 892733.
A traditional pottery with café on site as well as rare breed pigs, nature walks, three shops, play areas and 'have-a-go studio'. Home of the 'Collectible World Studios'.
Open all year, daily.

MARKETS
Appleby – Saturday

LATE-NIGHT FUEL
Davidson's Garage
Scotland Road, Penrith.
Telephone 01768 862456.
Open until midnight.

24-HOUR BREAKDOWN
Eden Garage
Temple Sowerby, Nr Penrith.
Telephone 017683 61212.

Ullswater Road Garage
Ullswater Road, Penrith.
Telephone 01768 64546.

Neil Bousfield Motors
Cromwell Road, Penrith.
Telephone 01768 892727.

TOUR TEN
~
Richmond and Swaledale

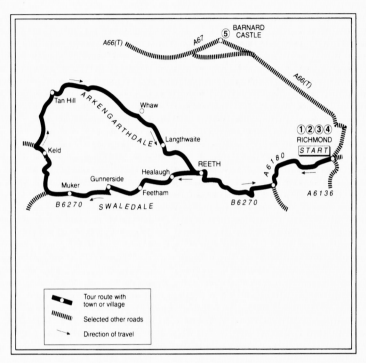

MAPS
OS Landranger nos. 91, 92, 98
OS Touring Map 6
The Yorkshire Dales

RECOMMENDED ACCOMMODATION
The Old Brewery Guest House
29 The Green, Richmond.
Telephone 01748 822460.

The Burgoyne Hotel
Reeth, Richmond.
Telephone 01748 884292.

Arkleside Hotel
Reeth, Richmond.
Telephone 01748 884200.

VISITOR ATTRACTIONS
1 Georgian Theatre Royal and
Museum
Victoria Road, Richmond.
Telephone 01748 823710 (Box
office – telephone 01748
823021).
One of the oldest theatres in the
country, with original stage sets
and playbills. It is still running as
a performing theatre. Open
Easter to October, every day; the
rest of the year, afternoons only.

2 Richmondshire Museum
Ryder's Wynd, Richmond.
Telephone 01748 825611.
Features the BBC TV set from
All Creatures Great and Small.
Open Easter to October, every
day, 10.30 am – 4.30 pm.

3 Green Howards Regimental
Museum
Trinity Church Square,
Richmond.
Telephone 01748 822133.
A museum dedicated to one of
Britain's oldest and most famous
regiments. Open April to
October, every day; closed

December and January; the rest
of year, open every day except
Sunday.

4 Richmond Castle
Tower Street, Richmond.
Telephone 01748 822493.
Open all year, daily.

5 Bowes Museum
Barnard Castle.
Telephone 01833 690606.
Slightly off the tour but one of
the North of England's premier
museums and art galleries. Open
all year, daily.

MARKETS
Richmond – Thursday and
Saturday

LATE-NIGHT FUEL
S.G. Petch Ltd.
Victoria Road, Richmond.
Telephone 01748 825757.
Open until 10.00 pm.

24-HOUR BREAKDOWN
Catterick Service Station
High Street, Catterick, Nr
Richmond.
Telephone 01748 811233.

TOUR ELEVEN
~
Malham and Littondale

MAPS
OS Landranger no. 98
OS Touring Map 6 The
Yorkshire Dales

RECOMMENDED ACCOMMODATION
The Amerdale House Hotel
Arncliffe, Littondale, Nr
Skipton.
Telephone 01756 770250.

Langcliffe Country House
Kettlewell.
Telephone 01756 760243.

VISITOR ATTRACTIONS
1 Yorkshire Dales Falconry and
Conservation Centre
Just off the A65, north of Settle.
Telephone 01729 825164.
Birds of prey from all over the
world, including a magnificent
Andean Condor with a ten-foot
wingspan. Flying demonstrations
throughout the day and bird-
handling courses are available.
Tea room, gift shop and
children's playground. If the
weather is poor, ring first to
check if flying demonstrations
can take place. Open Easter to
October, daily. Call for winter
opening times.

2 Museum of North Craven
Life
North Craven Heritage Centre,
6 Chapel Street, Settle.
Telephone 01729 822854.
A museum specifically dedicated
to the story of rural life in the
area in the eighteenth and
nineteenth centuries, plus an
exhibition about the Settle to
Carlisle railway. Open Easter to
September, weekend afternoons
only, plus bank holidays; July and
August, every day.

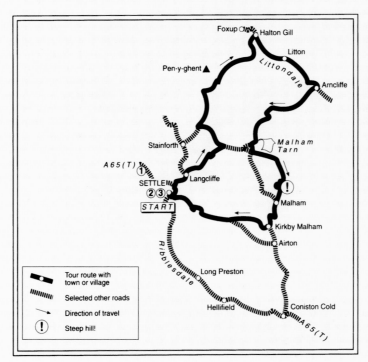

3 Craven Museum
Town Hall, High Street, Skipton.
Telephone 01756 706407.
A more general exhibition than
the above, covering Skipton and
the Dales from Roman times
onwards. Open April to
September, every day except
Tuesday; in winter, afternoons
only, closed Tuesday and Sunday.

CRAFT SHOPS
The Dalesmade Centre
Watershed Mill, Langcliffe Road,
Settle. Telephone 01729 825111.
The Dalesmade scheme
promotes locally crafted
products, Watershed Mill being
the first collection exclusively to
exhibit the range. Includes
furniture, carvings, cards, clocks,
sculpture, knitwear and more.
Also a good coffee shop.

Linton Court Gallery
Duke Street, Settle.

Telephone 01729 822695.
Contemporary art exhibitions.

The Malham Cove Centre
Malham. Telephone 017293 432.
Sells a range of local crafts and
woollens.

MARKETS
Settle – Tuesday

LATE-NIGHT FUEL
Ingfield Service Station
Skipton Road, Settle.
Telephone 01729 823009.
Open until 9.00 pm.

24-HOUR BREAKDOWN
The West Yorkshire Garage
47 Duke Street, Settle.
Telephone 01729 822529.

City Auto Repairs
2 Workshop, Mainway, Skerton,
Lancaster.
Telephone 01524 843880.

TOUR TWELVE
~
The Western Dales

MAPS
OS Landranger no. 98
OS Touring Map 6
The Yorkshire Dales

RECOMMENDED ACCOMMODATION
Stone Close
Dent.
Telephone 015396 25231.

VISITOR ATTRACTIONS
1 Holme Farm
Sedbergh.
Telephone 015396 20654.
A nature-trail and animal feeding on an open farm. Also a badger watch. Open March to September.

2 White Scar Caves
On the B6255, Hawes to Ingleton road.
Telephone 015242 41244.
A massive, 200,000-year-old cavern with a one-mile long guided tour. The caves are very well lit, with walk-ways and guide-rails. The tour lasts about eighty minutes and is well worth doing. Open all year, daily.

3 Ingleton Waterfall Walk
It is privately owned and tickets are available from the car-park at the start. Open all year.

Settle to Carlisle Railway.
Timetables available throughout the year. Contact the British Rail station at Carlisle for details.
Telephone 01228 44711.

CRAFT SHOPS
Curlew Crafts
Main Street, Ingleton.
Telephone 015242 41608.
Upmarket crafts and a nice café.

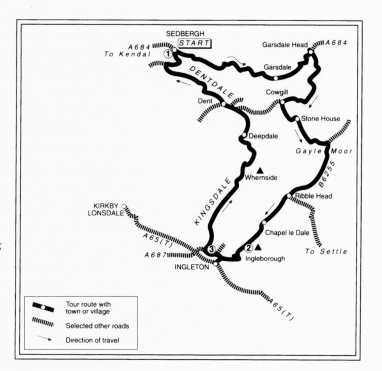

Dent Craft Centre
Helmside, Near Dent.
Telephone 015396 25400.
Unusual arts and crafts, many of them locally-made.
Demonstrations and a tea room.
Open Easter to early January, daily, also winter weekends.

MARKETS
Ingleton – Friday
Sedbergh – Wednesday

LATE-NIGHT FUEL
Three Peaks Services
A65 New Road, Ingleton.
Telephone 015242 41770.
Open 24 hours.

24-HOUR BREAKDOWN
Craven Recovery Services
Unit 1A, Ingleton Industrial Estate, New Road, Ingleton.
All callouts are handled by their Skipton branch, telephone 01756 798311.

TOUR THIRTEEN
~
Wharfedale, Middleham and Nidderdale

MAPS

OS Landranger nos. 98, 99
OS Touring Map 6
The Yorkshire Dales

RECOMMENDED ACCOMMODATION

47 Main Street, Grassington.
Telephone 01756 752069.

Ashfield House
Grassington.
Telephone 01756 752584.

Greystones
Market Place, Middleham.
Telephone 01969 622016.

Miller's House
Market Place, Middleham.
Telephone 01969 622630.

Waterford House
Kirkgate, Middleham.
Telephone 01969 622090.

Sportsman's Arms
Wath-in-Nidderdale,
Nr Pateley Bridge.
Telephone 01423 711306.

VISITOR ATTRACTIONS

1 The Upper Wharfedale Museum
6 The Square, Grassington.
Telephone 01756 753059.
The museum is housed in two eighteenth-century cottages, formerly lead-miners' homes. With plenty of local artefacts, the exhibition depicts the history and life of the area. Open afternoons only: Easter to September, every day; winter, weekends only.

2 Kilnsey Park
Kilnsey, Nr Grassington.
Telephone 01756 752150.
A privately-owned park with an aquarium, fishing, picnic area

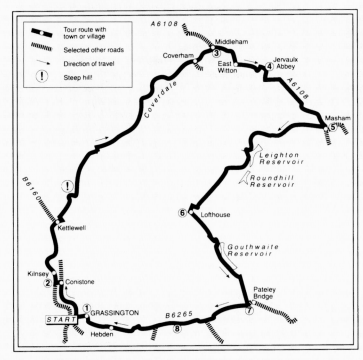

and a Dales-life visitor centre. Open all year, daily.

3 Middleham Castle
Middleham.
Telephone 01969 623899.
Currently in the care of English Heritage and one of the most interesting castles in the area. Open April to September, every day; winter, daily except Monday and Tuesday.

4 Jervaulx Abbey
Jervaulx.
Telephone 01677 460391.
Open all year, daily – admission by honesty box!

5 Theakston's Brewery Visitor Centre
Masham.
Telephone 01765 689057.
Open Easter to October, Wednesday to Monday; November to mid-December,

Wednesday, Saturday and Sunday only. Note that tours are available of the brewery at certain times (ring first to check).

6 How Stean Gorge
Lofthouse, Nidderdale.
Telephone 01423 755666.
A walk to the limestone gorge, plus a children's play area and café. Open all year, daily except Mondays and Tuesdays in January and February.

7 Nidderdale Museum
Pateley Bridge.
Telephone 01423 711225.
A fascinating museum, winner of the 1990 National Heritage Museum of the Year Award. Open Easter to October, every day 2.00–5.00 pm; October to Easter, weekend afternoons only.

8 Stump Cross Caverns
Greenhow, Pateley Bridge.

Telephone 01756 752780.
One of the best known show-caves in the area. Centre, café and shop on site. Open Easter to October, every day; winter, weekends only.

CRAFT SHOPS

Old School Arts Workshop
Top Cross, Middleham.
Telephone 01969 623056.
Modern sculpture and demonstration days. Also a gallery and a bookshop. Courses available.

Masham Pottery
Rear of King's Head Hotel,
Market Place, Masham.
Telephone 01765 689780.
A small local pottery producing a range of distinctive stoneware.

Uredale Glass
Market Place, Masham.
Telephone 01756 689780.
Traditional glass blowing and demonstrations.

MARKETS

Masham – Wednesday
Skipton – Monday, Wednesday, Friday and Saturday

LATE-NIGHT FUEL

Leyburn Garage
Middleham Road, Middleham.
Telephone 01969 622110.
Open until 8.00 pm.

Skipton Service Station
Keighley Road, Skipton.
Telephone 01756 700622.
Open 24 hours.

24-HOUR BREAKDOWN

Craven Recovery Services
Craven Garage, Engine Shed Lane, Skipton.
Telephone 01756 798311.

TOUR FOURTEEN
~
Hawes and Wensleydale

MAPS
OS Landranger no. 98
OS Touring Map 6
The Yorkshire Dales

RECOMMENDED ACCOMMODATION
Simonstone Hall Country House Hotel
Hawes.
Telephone 01969 667255.

Cocketts Hotel and Restaurant
Market Place, Hawes.
Telephone 01969 667312.

Stone House Guest House
Sedbusk.
Telephone 01969 667571.

VISITOR ATTRACTIONS
1 Dales Countryside Museum
Station Yard, Hawes.
Telephone 01969 667450.
Originally the Upper Dales Folk Museum, this has been recently refurbished by the National Park and now contains an excellent exhibition reflecting the rural life of the area. Open Easter to October, every day; November, weekends only; then open Christmas to New Year.

2 Bolton Castle
Wensleydale.
Telephone 01969 623981.
Attractively recreated rooms and a small museum and tearooms. Open March to November, every day.

3 Yorkshire Carriage Museum
Yore Mill, Aysgarth.
A private collection of horse-drawn carriages and vehicles. For information contact the National Park information centre at Aysgarth Falls. Open Easter to October, every day.

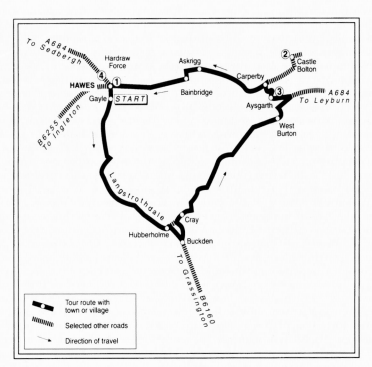

4 Hardraw Scar Waterfall
Green Dragon Inn, Hardraw, Nr Hawes.
Telephone 01969 667392.
A detour from the main route, but worth it to see England's highest single-drop waterfall. Access is via the Green Dragon Inn. Open all year, every day. Admission charge.

CRAFT SHOPS
Hawes Ropemakers
W.R. Outhwaite and Son, Hawes.
Telephone 01969 667487.
A traditional rope-making business where you can see it actually being made. Open Monday to Friday, all year; also Saturdays in summer.

Aysgarth Pottery
Aysgarth.
Telephone 01969 663719.

MARKETS
Hawes – Tuesday

LATE-NIGHT FUEL
S.G. Petch Ltd.
Victoria Road, Richmond.
Telephone 01748 825757.
Open until 10.00 pm.

TOUR FIFTEEN
~
The Forest of Bowland

MAPS
OS Landranger nos. 97, 98, 102, 103.

RECOMMENDED ACCOMMODATION
Whoop Hall Inn
Burrow-with-Burrow,
Kirkby Lonsdale.
Telephone 015242 71284.

Cobwebs Country House and
Restaurant
Leck, Cowan Bridge,
Kirkby Lonsdale.
Telephone 015242 72141.

Hipping Hall
Cowan Bridge, Kirkby Lonsdale.
Telephone 015242 71187.

Hark To Bounty Inn
Slaidburn.
Telephone 01200 446246.

Parrock Head Hotel
Slaidburn.
Telephone 01200 446614.

VISITOR ATTRACTIONS
The tour itself is remarkably
devoid of commercial attractions,
which in some ways contributes
to its charm. However, if it's wet
or you fancy a day among the
bright lights, it's worth a detour
into Lancaster.

1 The Ashton Memorial
Williamson Park, Lancaster.
Telephone 01524 33318.
Nikolaus Pevsner called it 'the
greatest monument in England'.
It contains an exhibition devoted
to Lord Ashton on the ground
floor. There is a splendid
butterfly-house inside and an
aviary outside. Open Easter and
May to September, every day;
open daily during October to
158

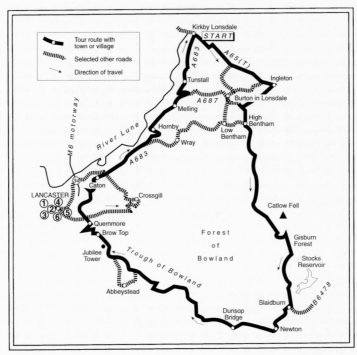

April but with restricted hours.
Admission is free to the park and
the ground-floor exhibition.

2 Promenade in the Park
Williamson Park is the host to a
season of open-air plays during
the summer. A full programme
can be obtained from the
Lancaster Information Centre or
The Duke's Playhouse, telephone
01524 66645.

3 Lancaster Castle
Telephone 01524 64998.
Open Easter to the end of
October (subject to Crown
Court sittings in the building),
every day (scheduled tours
available).

4 Lancaster City Museum
Market Square, Lancaster.
Telephone 01524 64637.
Originally the Town Hall, this
impressive eighteenth-century
building now houses the city
museum and the museum of the
King's Own Regiment. Open all
year, Monday to Saturday.
Admission free.

5 Lancaster Maritime Museum
St George's Quay, Lancaster.
Telephone 01524 64637.
A relatively new museum,
opened in 1985, and sited in the
old customs house. There is a
café and shop on site. Open
April to October, daily;
November to March, afternoons
only.

6 Judges' Lodging Museum
Church Street, Lancaster.
Telephone 01524 32808.
Built as a private house in 1620,
it became a lodging house for
judges during the Lancaster
Assizes. It now has two separate
museums, one dedicated to
furniture and the other to

childhood. Open July to October
10.30 am–1 pm and 2 pm–5 pm;
2 pm to 5 pm only on Saturdays.
Open 2 pm to 5 pm Monday to
Saturday only for the rest of the
year.

CRAFT SHOPS
Bentham Pottery
Bentham, Nr Ingleton.
Telephone 015242 61567.
Stoneware and pottery, with
demonstrations and courses
available.

Brow Top Craft Centre
Quernmore, Nr Lancaster.
Telephone 01524 66833.
Craft shop and tea room.

MARKETS
Kirkby Lonsdale – Thursday

LATE-NIGHT FUEL
Three Peaks Services
A65 New Road, Ingleton.
Telephone 015242 41770.
Open 24 hours.

24-HOUR BREAKDOWN
Craven Recovery Services
Unit 1A, Ingleton Industrial
Estate, New Road, Ingleton.
All call-outs are handled by their
Skipton branch, telephone 01756
798311.

City Auto Repairs
2 Workshop, Main Way, Skerton,
Lancaster.
Telephone 01524 843880.

INDEX

~

Major entries are in **bold**, picture references in *italic*.

ACKNOWLEDGEMENTS

My thanks to everyone who has helped with the research and writing of this book, in particular: Viv Bowler, at Little, Brown, whose enthusiasm got the whole project on the road in the first place; Pam Williamson, for drawing my attention to the Solway Firth and for her exhaustive Dales research (and hello to Chris and Roy); Pam Grant and David Ward, for putting up with driving round and round in circles and doing the shopping; Bill Boumphrey, who didn't know quite what he was letting himself in for, when he brought his new XR3-something-or-other to the Lakes for the first time; my sister, Lorna, for checking text and typing up my notes; Eileen and Elwyn Morgan for details about Greystoke Castle; Lakeland Computer Services, Kendal, especially Rick Fry for courageously lending me his Apple PowerBook; the staff at the Cumbria Tourist Board, the Yorkshire and Humberside Tourist Board and the Lancaster Tourist Board; and finally, Elliot, for his unceasing efforts to find the best sticky toffee pudding in the Lake District. . . .

Colin Shelbourn